# Travel photography: A planner     uide

Planning and executing great travel ph

ames Dugan

www.walkaboutphotoguides.com

# Copyright and disclaimer

# READER BONUSES

As a thank you to readers of this guide, we have three bonus downloads for you that help in the preparation phase of your photo trips:

- **Photo shot list -** An example photo shot list to give you a base to create your own list. This comprehensive list includes a variety of standard scenarios, allowing you to customise the items to suit your trip.

- **Packing checklist -** Forgetting to pack something in your bags happens to the best of us and adding all of your camera gear only complicates life! This typical packing checklist gets you off to a great start and is customisable to your needs (no doubt this list will be tweaked over time).

- **How-to guide for Google Maps list -** Step-by-step (with screenshots) guide to creating a custom Google Maps list.

For your free bonuses, head over to
https://walkaboutphotoguides.com/travelphotosplanning/bonuses/

# ABOUT THIS GUIDE

The purpose of this guide is to help walk you through the planning and logistics that go into executing a productive and enjoyable trip to take photos. This trip can be as straightforward as visiting the next town over to take photos or jetting off halfway around the world. The core concepts remain the same wherever you go; only the complexity varies.

Taking a trip with the express intention of taking photos can be different to a regular trip in a few key ways, most of are influenced by chasing the best light on your subjects – good light is often the secret sauce to capturing a compelling image:

- **Timing** - Structure your visits to specific locations to coincide with the best light conditions. This means being able to be flexible with your schedule, particularly if you have to work with variable weather conditions.

- **Pacing** - Taking time to "work" a subject / location for the best images takes time. This is often a lot more than the average non-photographer travel companion is likely to be able to put up with!

- **Walking** - There is likely to be a fair bit of walking involved, which may take some getting used to, particularly if you don't normally exercise on a regular basis.

- **Early starts** - Getting up in time to photograph sunrise has two huge benefits – you capture some of the best light of the day on your surroundings, and you are often likely to have the place to yourself whilst everybody else is still in bed. Depending on the time of year, you will need to get up earlier than usual to be in position for a sunrise.

- **Sunset** - This can often overlap with dinner times, so eating earlier or later than normal is probably going to occur.

In many ways, a photo trip is quite self-indulgent as it doesn't really leave time to spend with others and cater to their needs. As such, it can also feel quite solitary as your itinerary can be at odds with the timings of people on holiday. This can sound off-putting to begin with. If this sounds a little intimidating to you, start out small with half-day or day trips to whet your appetite.

# CONTENTS

# FREQUENTLY ASKED QUESTIONS

The Frequently Asked Questions (FAQ) below allow you to dive straight into the guide, and also some reassurance that others are working through the same challenges.

**Q: I've never travelled by myself before. What do I need to be thinking about?**

A: Firstly, congratulations for embarking on what should be a life-transforming experience! Once you realise that you can explore the world by yourself, it will open up huge possibilities (and potentially become an addiction). So, in practical terms, have a read of the following to start things off:

- **Where to stay** (page 12) - You can delve into finding places to stay that will allow you to feel safe while you travel. Also have a look at managing your stay (page 76).

- **Administrative matters** (page 32) - Particularly helpful if you aren't used to thinking about some of the "behind the scenes" matters that can get taken care of by tour organisers / travel companions.

- **General travel photography tips** when on the road (page 68) - Some considerations to make sure that you enjoy yourself and come away with great photos as well.

**Q: How can I make sure that I get the best shots?**

A: So many factors affect the success of your trip, however you can stack the deck in your favour:

- **When to go** (page 11) - Know the season, and the best time of year to photograph your destination.

- **Practice** (page 21) - Get to know your equipment in as many shooting situations as possible, particularly those that are similar to where you're traveling.

- **Getting the shot on the day** (page 69) - Little tips and tricks to maximise the likelihood that you'll have some "keeper" images at the end of each day.

**Q: What's the best place to book flights or accommodation?**

A: We have provided links for some of the most popular aggregators (page 116).

**Q: Where can I find more information about specific cities / locations?**

A: There are several excellent resources available to help you learn about a destination and plan your trip. Check out the section on researching where to go (page 11) and what to see and do (page 13).

**Q: How can I work out what features my camera has, and how to use them?**

A: In this guide we provide an overview of camera features (page 22), and what they can do. However, if you want to understand more about your specific camera's functionality, the best place to start is the camera's manual. These are generally downloadable from the camera manufacturer's website.

**Q: What's the best lens to travel with?**

A: This is a very difficult question to answer without knowing where you are heading, and what you intend on taking travel photos of. The most basic answer is – taking any camera will put you in a great position to come away with at least some images! If you are looking for more detailed information, take a read of the camera reference guide section (page 21).

**Q: What do I need to take?**

A: Assuming that your question is non-camera related, have a look at the section on packing (page 51). We cover the camera equipment, as well as other accessories and clothing that will help you along the way.

**Q: How do I save my photos when traveling so that I don't lose them?**

A: We have a section dedicated to ways to manage your photos when you're traveling (page 101).

**Q: I'm about to post bunch of my travel photos on social media. Anything I should be aware of?**

A: To navigate the potential pitfalls of posting to social media, we've written a section covering things to keep an eye out for (page 84). Apart from this, consider that fewer photos can often be more powerful than 200 photos of the same scene. Your friends and family will thank you!

**Q: What do all those fancy camera terms mean?**

A: Photography, like most hobbies, has developed its own language for describing physical characteristics of the cameras, lenses, types of images, etc. We've provided a glossary of terms (page 107) to help here.

**Q: Do I need a visa for traveling?**

A: If you are heading outside of your country (i.e. somewhere that you'll need to carry a passport for), visas may become part of your trip planning. Check out the section on visas (page 32) and the overview of visa-waivers and other visa types (page 120).

**Q: Help! I've booked a trip, and my plane leaves in a few hours. What are the key points that I may need to focus on at this late stage?**

A: On your way to the airport, have a read of the following:

- **Planning each day** (page 68) - A load of points to consider as you plan out the detail of what you'll be doing each day that you're at your destination.

- **Transportation tips** (page 64) - This is particularly helpful if you aren't so keen on flying. It also gives you a few pointers for when you hit the ground and are setting yourself up in your accommodation.

- **Health and safety precautions** (page 140) - Some information about diseases and illnesses to look for, as well as general first aid items that you can pick up at the airport on the way.

**Q: How come there are no photos in this travel photography guide?!?**

A: The focus of this guide is on the planning and logistics of travel photography. It may look glamorous when you see the finished product, however it's key to understand what goes on behind the scenes to make it all happen. This is the piece of the puzzle that can often get neglected. This guide will arm you with knowledge, and you and your camera(s) will be then able to focus (no pun intended!) getting great photos when you're at your destination.

We are publishing separate guides for several travel photography destinations around the globe. Check out our website (www.walkaboutphotoguides.com) for more information.

# PLANNING

# RESEARCH

## WHERE TO GO

This is a very subjective question; however, let's assume that you're choosing destinations from your photography (or travel) bucket list (page 115). Or perhaps, it is a collection of those recommendations from friends, colleagues, family, celebrities, news articles, etc. Make sure that you've got an idea which sites you want to see at the destination. You can also consider whether multiple bucket list items can be combined into one trip.

It is a good idea to have a system in place for adding ideas to your list, such as writing them down in a notebook, or creating a "To Do" list.

If all else fails, and you can't find inspiration for where to go, leave it to a degree of change. Go onto a flight aggregator website (page 118) and search for all flights leaving from your nearest airport. Pick one, and away you go. There is a definite appeal of capturing the serendipitous moments in life.

## WHEN TO GO

Seasonal changes bring unique photographic opportunities, in some cases transforming otherwise dreary locations into majestic vistas. Or, rendering a place of beauty into a heaving mass of humans. Some locations are renowned for a particular season, such as the Northern states of the United States when leaves change colours during the brief fall (autumn) season, or Kyoto in Japan for the cherry blossom season in spring each year. Not only will it be easier to reproduce the iconic shots that you may have seen, you're also more likely to be surrounded by like-minded people.

Speaking of crowds, they can have a huge impact on when you may choose to go. Cities like Venice can become almost unbearable in the height of summer, not only because of the weather but also because it's the peak tourist season.

If the idea of walking around all day in the baking sun doesn't quite appeal to you, consider visiting during a cooler time of the year. It will be less of a heat endurance test, and so you are also less likely to have to compete with others to get a good shot.

Assuming that you're not looking to visit a location for a specific event (e.g. Aspen for ski season), here are some factors to consider when deciding what might be the best time of the year for your trip:

- **Weather -** If a place is known for its beaches, then the middle of winter time may not be a great time for beach bums to visit. On the other hand, if you are a photographer looking for shots of open swathes of sand, pristine conditions, and clear waves, don't be afraid to go against the trend and visit during the off season.

- **Flight costs -** Airlines are very in tune with the peak and off-season of a location and will unashamedly price flights accordingly. If you're getting a deal, it is most likely that it is the off- season.

- **Hotel prices -** Similar to the point above, hotels also know when they can charge premium. However, be careful with using prices as your only gauge, as hotels can often close their doors to guests for months in the off season. Those hotels that choose to remain open can charge what the market shall bear.

# WHERE TO STAY

There are a lot of considerations to take when choosing where you want to stay for a photo trip. Fortunately, most places that you can visit do have a wide range of options (unless you leave booking to the last minute).

Here are some ways to choose the ideal hotel for your purpose. This also applies to other forms of paid accommodation as well.

## Being close to the action

The primary benefit of being close to the places you want to see is that you can be more efficient with your time, allowing you to be in a specific place during critical times of the day for photos. Getting out of bed in time for sunrise may be a little more appealing if you don't have to then travel far. And at the end of the day, you don't have as far to go to get back to the comfort of a bed.

However, as the law of supply and demand states, if the "action" you are seeking happens to be the same as other people (i.e. the demand), you will have to vie for a room (the supply). I is also most likely that hotels will charge more because they can get away with it, and often position it as an "experience" as much as a practicality.

## Staying further out and using public transportation

As a general rule, the further out of town you are staying, the cheaper the accommodation. It is a good alternative for those on a budget, particularly if most of your activities are not limited at the city centre.

You are also able to stay someplace that is quieter, allowing a bit of much-needed sleep. However, you need to consider public transportation if you decided to stay outside the city, unless you're staying somewhere that has cheap taxi services.

## Walking distances

When evaluating your itinerary and accommodation, you also need to consider how much walking may be required. Separately, take into account the time of year that you are traveling, as the temperature outside may not be pleasant for long stretches of walking (tropical summer or winter snow). In some places, you may only want to be outdoors for 5-10 minutes at a time to avoid heat stroke or freezing.

## Safety of the area

Tourism zones in most destinations tend to be patrolled by police or private security services and are generally considered safe. The same could not be said of your hotel location; thus, you have to factor in getting taxis to / from your hotel to the tourist area (or where you want to visit). If in doubt about the safety of the area, check the online reviews of the hotel. As a guide, luxury hotel chains can be found in most parts of the world and usually found in the safer parts of a town. So even if you don't stay at a luxury hotel, if you stay in the same area it should be a safer option.

## Use Google Street view (or similar)

A relatively simple way to get a feel for an area is to use a tool such as Google Street view. Based on this, you can get some indication as to whether the place looks safe, although bear in mind that photos will be taken in the day in good light. Using such tools also allow you to assess the veracity of claims of a hotel about the "views" that you might be able to get from rooms or the roof terrace. In some cases, "city view" can actually mean, "you'll see the building on the other side of the alley".

## Stay in multiple hotels in the same city during your trip

This can feel a little tricky, however staying in multiple parts of a city can be the ninja move that allows you to easily reach all of your intended destinations with minimal fuss. Moving hotels during the day isn't generally too difficult, and often it's the time of the day where light is the least flattering for a lot of subjects anyway.

# WHAT TO SEE

There is more to explore in a city than the one iconic structure or popular festival that is taking you there. Here are some approaches to planning what to do on your trip.

# Don't try to cram it all in during one trip

You can always return to the places you have visited! Keep this in mind, and you are more likely to have a relaxing time which will allow you to focus on quality over quantity. Limitations to the idea of being able to return are typically limited to:

- **Geopolitical changes** - war, civil unrest, or changes in government can make places that were once open to tourism become difficult or impossible to visit. Or more nascently, the government of the destination location has made it more difficult for citizens of your country to obtain visas.

- **Destruction / erosion** - sadly, famous places can and do deteriorate over time. Some can either completely disappear, or people can be restricted from entry. A famous example of this is the pyramids of Giza, which once were accessible including climbing to the top!

- **Budget** - some places like Easter Island, Antarctica, or the North Pole are usually "once in a lifetime" destinations owing to the expensive cost of getting there and back.

- **There isn't actually that much to see / photograph** - unlike all of the above reasons, this is somewhat more subjective. If there are only a few things to see, you can cover them in your first visit of a few days instead of returning. You're more likely to come to this conclusion once you're on the ground.

# Where to find information / search terms

Here are some ways to find more information about the place that you're intending to visit:

## Animals and birds

If you're looking for cute photos of kittens and puppies, look no further than Instagram. If you're interested in a wider variety of animals, look for the following places in your chosen destination:

- Zoos and animal sanctuaries are excellent places to see animals of all shapes and sizes up close.
- Wildlife parks / wetlands areas - these may require greater patience and better timing, however you'll have the satisfaction of capturing animals "in the wild".

## Architecture

Your interest in architecture for a location may be for specific building / style, a period of history, or the general feel of a location. The following are ways to help build a list of places to check out:

- Look for "{*destination*} famous buildings".

- Google Maps, including Google Street View, to home in on whether the buildings are in line with your expectations (to justify a trip).

## Costumes / clothing

Depending on the location, traditional clothing may be worn all of the time, or only donned for festivals. For example, you are going to encounter people wearing traditional *kimono* outfits in major Japanese cities on any given day (often just to pose for photos). However, you'd only expect to see Munich residents bedecked in *lederhosen* during the *Oktoberfest* festival. Check out the Festivals section below for more information.

If your interest lies in period costume, armour, special garments, etc. then check out the following in your chosen destination:

- Arts and / or design museums
- War museums
- Museums (general)
- Monuments / Historic buildings
- Historical societies

## Festivals

Assuming that the festival is not a one-time event, the following ways can help you find out details for festivals and what conditions may exist for taking photos:

- Look for "{*destination*} festival", or "{*destination country*} national holidays".
- Travel agencies should also be able to tell you about major festivals in a location.

## Food / drink / local traditions

A core feature of most cultures the food and drink consumed by locals, and invariably is closely tied to local traditions as well. It is a great way to bring depth to photo stories from your trips. Check out the following for types of food / drink to seek out:

- Cookbooks specialising in the cuisine of the country / location of interest
- Restaurant reviews for the destination, as simple as looking for "{*destination*} restaurant review"
- Beer - "{*destination*} brewery"
- Whisky / gin - "{*destination*} distillery"
- Wine - "{*destination*} winery"

## Historical locations / history

If you are looking for "generalist" history for a location, the following can be great resources:

- Museums
- National monuments / war memorials
- Historical societies

## Landscapes and nature

Usually, the landscape is the destination in itself, such as lakes, national parks, and mountain ranges. If you're heading to a built-up area, or you are unsure about your destination, look online for search terms including "viewpoint", "landscape", "nature" and "park".

## Natural events

Natural events run the gamut of phenomena from Northern (and Southern) lights, solstices, eclipses, king tides, and seasonal flooding. Some great resources for learning more about where to capture natural events in an area are:

- Geographic societies
- Astronomical societies
- National parks services

## People

Assuming you're looking for something more specific than "people walking down the street", the following places / events are going to improve your odds of capturing people in action:

- Festivals / special events (see above) - it might be an idea to plan your whole trip around an event that you want to be present for. Crowds will form, often wearing traditional dress. Look for public holidays in the location that you're visiting, as they tend to coincide with big events.
- Town squares which are often located near train stations, city halls, or other places of cultural significance.
- Public transport hubs, including bus depots, main train stations, airports, seaports / piers.
- Markets, including fresh produce, flea markets, etc. Permanent markets tend to operate all week, otherwise weekends are more likely to be busy (and so more people to photograph).

# CAPTURING YOUR RESEARCH

## Inspiration

We usually see and hear things that are going to trigger a desire to visit certain places. Having a habit of writing down travel ideas (plus what you want to do when you are there) will not only help in formulating a plan for an upcoming trip but will also provide a great go-to when it's time for your trip.

Depending on your interests and style of travel, consider saving the information that you collect by city or country. Grouping together images, articles, reviews, etc. by theme may be helpful but it can be harder to move from this information into planning an actual trip. For example, capturing information on "cats" might be an endless source of fascination however make sure to sort the information in a coherent manner so you can readily access your notes on places to visit to see "cats".

The following are suggestions for easily collating your travel inspirations digitally (excluding word processors and spreadsheets):

- **Evernote or Microsoft OneNote -** Capture emails, links to articles, photos, thoughts, reviews by friends and family, lists, etc. You are able to add narration on any of the information you collated. These tools work offline.

- **Pinterest -** Online portal used for creating impressions and mood boards. This can help collate inspiration from different places, including images, articles, etc.

- **Email -** Create email folders for filing ideas and recommendations. Images and links can be emailed to yourself to file away.

Going a very different direction, there is something powerful about using physical ways of capturing your travel photography desires. Having this information placed somewhere in your house / office that you are going to see regularly can continue to motivate you to get a trip underway or inspire you to plan out the travel year. Some suggestions:

- **Map of the country / map of the world -** Use pins to colour-code places visited, and places to visit.

- **Scrapbook -** While it may feel old-fashioned to some, the act of cutting-and-pasting articles that you've read from newspapers and magazines and placing them into a scrapbook is more likely to make you start visualising and planning that trip.

- **Pinboard -** Similar to scrapbooking, substituting pins for glue.

# Planning

Having a system for capturing down your inspiration, and subsequent research, can help enormously when it comes time to plan a trip. Using Evernote or OneNote to plan allows more dynamic reordering of information as a plan comes together. This tends to be more efficiently than other means.

Key information to write down when planning locations to visit:

## Opening hours

Take note of opening hours as well as opening days of the week. Museums often are closed on a Monday in many cities, places of worship are closed for services on specific days of the week (Sundays for Christian churches), and parks can have seasonal closures. For countries in the Middle East, the weekend is Friday and Saturday, with many places closed on a Friday

## Costs

The costs of the trip can start mounting, especially if there are lots of places at the destination that charge entry fees. Most tourist destinations have created multi-pass pricing structures that both help make the total cost of visits cheaper, as well as provide a bit of an incentive to visit less-popular locations by virtue that you've already "paid" for access with the multi-pass.

Multi-pass type plans can take the form of "Museums", "Churches", or general attractions. In addition, multi-day passes can be tied in with public transport passes as well. Consider your travel plans as an unlimited public transport option can often work out quite cost effective.

## Locations / addresses

It's important to understand where specific places you want to visit are located in relation to each other. You can gauge this through marking on a map or creating a Google Maps list (page 75). Through this exercise you can determine how you will get around a location, be it by foot, public transportation, or other means. You may need to consider hiring a car / bike to reach places that are outside of a city centre or look further into public transport arrangements.

# YOUR PHOTO SHOT LIST

A photo shot list is the check list that you create to ensure that you know what photos you are looking to take during a project / trip. Having a shot list makes everything feel that much more efficient when you are on the ground. It also allows you to come away from a trip being comfortable that you've captured the photos that you set out for.

# Bringing it all together

We covered inspiration earlier (page 17), and perhaps during this time there were specific photos that captured your imagination. For best results, keep the check list concept in mind, including being able to check off completed items. For each item on the photo shot list, make sure you capture the following:

- **Location / area** - Where you expect to take the photo.

- **Time** - Record the time of day, and perhaps the day of week for places that are only open on weekends (for example). You can group shots together if they have time bounds (and are nearby).

- **Lens choice** - If you know in advance, note down what camera lens you think you may need, particularly for larger lens. This way you may choose to group the photos that require a big and heavy lens together to take at one time so that you don't have the lug the lens around for the rest of the trip.

Suggested ways to create your shot list:

- **Image gallery / mood board -** Each item to tick off is an image that has been sourced from the information collected during the inspiration phase.

- **Written list -** Document your list with as much descriptive information as possible.

- **Map with markers -** This can be through use of Google Maps lists (page 75) or simply marking the places you want to visit on a map.

You can always adopt a combination of the above suggestions as well, to suit your needs. Experiment with different options, and you'll find a solution that works best for you.

# Making it accessible during your trip

Regardless of the approach that you take, your shot list needs to be accessible throughout each day that you are on the ground. If the solution(s) that you are using isn't electronic, consider taking photos of it on your phone so that you can scroll through during the day.

> **Tip:** Ensure that your shot list is accessible offline, as you may not have Internet access all of the time, including indoor locations. This means that you are never caught out and unable to review your shot list.

**Bonus:** To help bring this to life, we have created a comprehensive photo shot list that caters for a variety of scenarios that you are likely to encounter when traveling. We've incorporated several of the approaches suggested above, and it's designed so that you can modify it to your needs.

To get your free photo shot list, head over to
walkaboutphotoguides.com/travelphotosplanning/bonuses

# PRACTISING YOUR TECHNIQUE

We have spent a fair bit of time discussing the planning of logistics of the trip, and now we need to bring our focus back to the reason why we are going in the first place – great photos. The old axiom of "practice makes perfect" applies to pretty much every facet of life. The mountaineer doesn't set out to climb Mount Everest without first wearing in their boots and becoming intimately comfortable with the equipment that they are going to be using.

Similarly, for you as a travel photographer, learning how to best use your equipment and apply technique under calm / low risk situations will give you an edge for when you're in the field, and the stakes are a little higher. As such, it is important to ensure familiarity with your equipment in addition to technique (which generally can be applied to any equipment). To get the best shots possible, practice and experience with both are your way forward (and great light!).

You may be wondering why should you invest the time and effort in practising at home (or near home) rather than out in the field? Perhaps one way to approach this can be from a value of time standpoint. If you are working in a regular salary job, you are able to determine what each of your annual leave days is worth to you in terms of cash (even if you can't necessarily sell your annual leave days). On top of this is the fact that you've spent the time and (sometimes) emotional energy in getting to a location, you would want to get the best bang for your buck. If you are comfortable with your technique beforehand, you are much more likely to be efficient when you're traveling.

The second way to think about the value of practice at home is that you are going to be better placed to capture those fleeting moments that will occur when you are photographing moving objects (people, animals, weather, nature). These moments may not present themselves very often, so it's harder to practice, no matter where you are. Knowing what settings to have on your camera, and what compositional techniques that will bring out the best of the scene, will help you to come away from a trip happy.

So whilst practicing at home may feel a little silly, or even contrived, it is an investment that you're making in your personal development as a travel photographer.

# FAMILIARITY WITH YOUR CAMERA AND EQUIPMENT

Photography is a hobby (and profession) that has a propensity to encourage what is often termed Gear Acquisition Syndrome (GAS). Having GAS is a scenario where the allure of the latest shiny device becomes irresistible. Some people can get to a point of being able to justify in their minds that this new piece of equipment will somehow become the key to unlocking their awesome photographic abilities! At the risk of bursting bubbles for some, GAS does tend to have associated afflictions - "Buyer's remorse" and "Hefty credit card bill"!

Most of us can come to terms with the idea that driving a Ferrari won't, of itself, make you a better driver. This statement doesn't bely the fact that having a bright red Ferrari in the driveway will make you the envy of your friends, and make you feel super confident! And if you are a very good driver, a Ferrari will allow you to push the limits of your driving potential more so than a "sensible" car ever could. So, go ahead and buy the Ferrari, or the shiny new camera or lens – just make sure that the reasons for your purchase is clear in your mind!

Cameras and lenses are tools. At the end of the day, they are tools that help translate your vision of a scene into a reality that can be shared with others. Let's talk a little bit about how that will all come together.

# Camera functions

The different modes on your camera exist to serve different purposes, depending on the situation that you are capturing. Becoming familiar with which mode can help bring your vision to life is where some time needs to be spent. For greater detail on what each mode does, refer to the reference section (page 92). Having some experience with each mode will not only give insight into which mode(s) is most appropriate for a situation, you'll also become more familiar with how your camera will respond.

Apart from reading the camera's manual to have an overall understanding of its performance, consider spending more time on understanding how the following functions work (if your camera offers them):

### High Dynamic Range (HDR) / auto-bracketing settings

The human eye is capable of seeing a wider range of light than any camera in existence today. A simple way to visualise this is to think of a scene where you are standing in front of the inside window of a dark house, on a sunny day. A human eye can see definition in the shadows under the window as well as the brightly lit scenery outside of the window. Cameras will struggle with getting all of this detail without blowing the highlights (brightest part of the image) or not capturing enough definition in the shadows.

HDR photographs look to overcome this camera limitation by combining multiple exposures of the same image, with each exposure taking in a difference range of light (normal, the bright areas, and the dark areas). These images can be then used to create a final image that better resembles that dynamic range that your eyes can see.

Your camera will have bracketing options that will automatically adjust the camera's exposure settings to take multiple images back-to-back. Settings can include choosing how many images to take, whether to shoot continuously (i.e. holding the shutter button down will take all of the photos in succession) or not, and how wide an exposure range to capture which is measured in "stops". A typical setting for auto-bracketing is "-2 stops", "normal", "+2 stops", often denoted in the camera as "-2,-,+2".

> **Tip:** For best results, use Aperture priority mode when using auto-bracketing. This will keep the aperture of each of the exposures the same, which is crucial for being able to combine the images in post-processing. If possible, if you have good light or are using a tripod, fix the ISO to a low value as well. This will produce the least noisy images, and so your camera will only vary the shutter speed for each exposure shot.

## Auto-ISO

Depending on which camera mode you are in, your camera will vary the ISO for a shot as part of getting the correct exposure. If the light is less than optimal, the camera will attempt to increase the ISO as its first priority. Bear this in mind if you are trying to get low-noise photos, as you may wish to consider changing the aperture setting instead.

## Focusing modes

Modern cameras have several focusing modes that can be used, utilising a combination of the information detected by the camera's sensor and intelligence in the camera's software to determine what the camera should focus on. This is what auto-focus modes tend to do, and mostly this works.

If you are wanting to be more precise about what is in greatest focus, you can use spot-metering on what is in the middle of the camera's viewfinder. Understanding the radius that the spot focusing will cover is important, so that can predict what the camera will focus on.

For the most precise focus, switch your camera (and lens in many cases) to "manual focus" mode. Use the magnification preview feature of the camera to electronically zoom in on what you want to focus in so ensure you get the tightest focus possible.

## Focus tracking

This can be a complex concept to master, particularly understanding how your camera will follow a moving object. In addition, understanding the limitations of focus tracking is important, including how much of the camera's frame can be used for focus-tracking. Stand-in moving objects to practice focus tracking can include young children, pets, and passing cars in the street.

## High ISO noise

The higher the ISO, the "noisier" the image. Depending on the situation, and the published size of the image, this may or may not be an issue. If you are shooting for thumbnails, or small-size web images / Instagram, then you are likely to have a fairly high tolerance for noise as it won't be visible in small images. However, if you're a "pixel peeper" (zooming in to every part of the image to look at quality), you are much more likely to seek out low-ISO images.

Understanding the maximum acceptable ISO of an image before noise becomes intolerable (a very subjective point) is important to enable you to get pleasing shots in low-light conditions. Noise is most apparent in dark areas / shadows, so practice shooting indoors or times when noise is mostly going to show up. For most cameras, shooting up to ISO 1600 will produce very acceptable images, and the bigger the camera's sensor, generally the higher the ISO that will be acceptable. For modern full frame cameras, images shot at up to ISO 6400 (or even beyond) are generally acceptable quality even when zoomed in. High ISO on phone cameras tends to be incredibly noisy (due to small camera sensor size) and is likely to be an option of last resort for most people.

**Tip:** Despite what is said here about noise, often getting a noisy shot can be better than no shot at all. Travel photography is often about compromise!

## Time lapse

Taking photos at a defined interval is a great way to show the passage of time. Bear in mind that the more images that are taken, the bigger the drain on the camera's battery. Also think about the rate of change of whatever you're photographing – clouds don't vary much from one second to the next, however they do change minute to minute.

If you are able to control the location of the camera, you could create a time lapse that spans days / weeks / seasons. Technically this isn't using the time lapse functionality, rather returning to the same location at different times to take the photo.

## White balance

Adjusting the white balance will produce images in the same colour palette as what your eye will see. Your eyes are very good at compensating for different lighting conditions. If you are shooting in Raw, the white balance that you set in the camera will have zero effect on the Raw image. However, if you are shooting in JPEG, the camera may not always select the correct white balance, leaving your photos looking either too blue or too yellow.

Cameras will have suggested white balance settings to take advantage of typical indoor and outdoor light conditions. If you are shooting a scene with multiple different sources of light (e.g. sun and fluorescent light), it might be easier to shoot in Raw and adjust the white balance to a good compromise in post-processing.

## Noise reduction

Your camera can do all sorts of digital trickery to try to remove digital noise from images. In addition to changing the ISO settings (discussed above), noise reduction often involves taking multiple images in very quick succession. The camera's software will then average the pixels in these photos to smooth out the effect of random noise. Note that this feature in a camera is typically only applied to JPEG files as it is technically a form of post-processing.

Another way that a camera will look to remove noise for long exposure photos (usually with a shutter speed over one second) is to close the mirror and viewfinder, and then take an additional "black" image of the closed shutter (i.e. no image). The black image helps provide baseline for noisy pixels on the sensor, typically caused by heat. The two images are combined, and this simple treatment is applied to the final image that is saved and is a process that can be applied to Raw files as well as JPEG.

## Image sizes

Unless you are ABSOLUTELY desperate for memory card space, shoot at the largest image size that is possible in your camera. Photojournalists may have specific requirements to control image sizes in the interest of speed, however for travel photographers this should not be a consideration. Smaller image sizes mean that you are throwing away pixels, as you always have the option to shrink an image after the fact.

## Exposure compensation

This may be a feature that you're already comfortable using, however the camera may be set up to perform exposure compensation using different controls depending on which shooting mode you are in. Knowing how your camera allows you to adjust exposure in each camera mode is key, and you may be able to adjust these settings in your camera's menu system.

## Histogram

A histogram is a graphical representation of the spread of luminance (similar to brightness) across an image, from the shadows (on the left) to the highlights (on the right). The histogram is incredibly useful in determining whether an image is correctly exposed, from a technical standpoint. You may wish to introduce some artistic flair into the photo, making it naturally over- or under-exposed depending on the situation (e.g. silhouettes against sunset).

**Advanced tip:** The camera's histogram typically is based on a JPEG rendering of an image, even if shooting in Raw. This can mean that the camera may flag areas that are over-exposed when in fact you can still completely recover the highlights in post-processing. This is similar for shadows and darker areas of the image. Experiment with what the histogram on the camera's LCD shows you (i.e. a JPEG representation) compared with loading the image into an editor on your PC / Mac which will show you the actual Raw histogram data.

## LCD / viewfinder vs reality of images

Images that could look amazing on your camera's LCD may look much less so in reality. This is usually the case when shooting in Raw, as the image shown on the LCD is a JPEG rendering of the image (i.e. the image has had some post-processing performed by the camera). LCD images tend to compress the dark and light elements of a shot, and so the image can end up looking darker on the LCD than when viewing on a proper monitor.

## Back-button focusing

(This is an advanced approach). Back-button focusing is this is where the camera's focusing mechanism is de-coupled from the shutter button; pushing the shutter button will have no effect on the camera's focus. Enabling back-button focusing will mean that your camera will no longer operate the way most people expect a camera to work (i.e. point and shoot). You will have much more control of what is in focus when you take the shot, however you will need to separately focus the image first.

The "back button" refers to the button(s) on the back of the camera that can be set to do spot focusing or tracking focusing. Using back button focusing means that your camera will focus predictably regardless of changes in the scene in front of you (e.g. the focus won't suddenly latch onto a different object when you push the shutter button). It takes practice to be comfortable with this technique, so allow time to come to terms with it.

# Reducing blurry images

Sadly, this will be a familiar situation for all photographers. When you go to take the shot, everything looks like it set up correctly for what should be an amazing photo. That evening when you download the photo onto your computer, you discover that the image is shaky, or blurry. This can be a horrible feeling and can leaving you doubting both your competence as a photographer, and whether it's time to replace your gear (see earlier point about GAS!). However, consider the following approaches and techniques first to see if you can improve your odds of a good photo:

## Shutter speed

An old golden rule to getting the sharpest image possible (considering the light and other conditions) was to apply the rule of shutter speed equal to 1 / focal length. For example, if you were shooting at 50mm, make sure that your shutter speed is 1/50 sec or faster.

If you REALLY want to set yourself up for success, try and doubling this rule, so 1/100 sec in our example. This might feel like overkill, and practice will help you work out what is the minimal shutter speed you can get away with. This technique is most helpful when you don't quite have the time to stabilise your camera as much as possible, or you are shooting a fluid situation.

## Good stance

The more solidly you plant yourself, the greater the odds of your body being rigid when it comes to taking a photo. This can mean standing with your feet apart, or resting against a large object (tree, pole, building) to stabilise your body.

## Holding your camera

The act of pressing down the shutter button can have a rotational force effect as the right index finger pushes down on the shutter button. To reduce the chances of moving the camera when pressing the shutter, make sure that your camera and lens are supported in our left hand (this is described for a right-handed shooter) such that your right hand is not weight bearing at all. This means that you can wave your right hand about and your camera hasn't moved anywhere.

## Pressing the shutter button

Similar to using the trigger on a gun, a slow and smooth action is least likely to introduce movement into the camera when taking a photo. Don't be tempted to jab at the shutter button, rather try to roll your finger onto the button. This doesn't come easily to most people, and so should be practiced at home or where there are low stakes. An alternative strategy can be to use the 2-second shutter delay feature (present on most cameras) and ready the camera in anticipation of the shot. This removes the vibration effect of your finger on the shutter button.

## Shoot in continuous mode

Most cameras have the ability to shoot in a short burst mode, where multiple photos can be taken each second (measured in frames per second, or fps). You don't necessarily need to use the highest fps setting on your camera, however taking multiple shots at once increases your chances of one of the photos being sharp.

In general, especially for moving objects, apply the mantra of "if it's good enough to take one photo, then it's good enough to take two" (or even more). This is crucial when taking portraits of groups of people, as getting everyone looking in the same direction with eyes open and smiling can feel like herding a bunch of cats!

## Camera sensor and lens dust

Whilst technically dust issues won't cause blurry images, they are going to negatively affect the image quality consistently. Use a lens cloth regularly during the day to clean the front of the lens. When fitting a lens, make sure that you use the lens cloth to clean the rear of the lens as well. Use a lens blower (page 53) to help remove camera sensor dust.

## Sub-optimal aperture selected

This suggestion is slightly less about blurry photos, rather about generally out-of-focus shots. Lenses typically perform at their sharpest when they are used at two stops from their maximum. In English, if your lens is a f/2.8 at 50mm, it typically provides its sharpest images at f/5.6 (two stops). Low aperture values of f/16 and onwards are good for getting large depth of field, however this can be at the expense of image quality.

# TRIPODS

No other photography accessory has the ability to elevate the quality of your photos quite like what a tripod can do for you. This applies to the traditional three-legged tripods, mini tripods such as a Joby Gorilla Pod, as well as monopods.

Even using everyday objects to balance your camera will open up photographic opportunities that can make your images much more appealing. A tripod (or camera mount) paves the way for the world of long exposure photography, which is a boon in low-light situations or at night.

On the flipside of all of this greatness, the tripod has the propensity to also be the piece of travel photography gear that can be the heaviest, most cumbersome, unwieldly, attention-seeking, and most unwanted. It can often take quite some time to set up for most people. It's highly recommended to become comfortable with actually getting the tripod out, setting up, and getting a shot, and not being so bothered about the world around you.

Learning how to quickly set up and collapse your tripod is a great skill to have in your arsenal of photographic tricks. It also means that you can be quickly set up, get the shot, and packed up and away before security has the chance to start getting upset about using tripods in a place where it may not always be appreciated (if not outright banned).

> **Tip:** Practice getting all set up with your camera ready to go, and then packing up again, in a space at home. Practice this enough time that you are comfortable that you can do it in your sleep / in the dark (which may actually come up!).

> **Tip:** Make sure that you turn off any vibration reduction, In-Built Image Stabilisation (IBIS) or other similar capabilities that your camera body and / or lens has activated when using a tripod. These functions tend to get confused by the stability of a tripod and can start doing unexpected things that can mess up your shot.

> **Advanced tip:** If fitted to your tripod, look for a mounting hook on the centre column of your tripod, the column where you mount the camera. Hang your camera bag (or heavy weight) off it. This will help further stabilise your tripod by bringing the centre of gravity lower to the ground. It also allows you to easily access pockets in your camera bag to get hold of accessories.

# FLASHES

A well-placed flash (or multiple flashes) illuminates your subjects and can help you focus attention onto specific subjects in a photo. A flash isn't generally used for most forms of travel photography; however, they do come into their own when taking portraits. How to get the most out of your flash is an involved topic, and is outside of the scope of what we are going to cover here.

A flash is not a replacement for the sun! Most flashes will not light up entire buildings or objects 200 metres away – they aren't designed to do so, and the laws of physics are working against them. This point sadly has to be made here, as there are plenty of people wandering around with their on-camera flash going off at night to in a vain attempt to illuminate the darkness. Your two real options are to use a much more powerful flash or fixed light (and know its limitations) or use a tripod to allow for a longer-exposure.

**Tip:** If you must use the on-camera flash (which generally produces hideous images because of its harsh front-on nature), use some form of diffuser to soften the light. This could be as simple as a piece of white tissue or paper, a spent piece of film, or a white cloth or fabric.

# IMPROVING YOUR TECHNIQUE

Referring back to the analogy above about the Ferrari not making you a better driver, you are going to realise greater improvements in your images as you improve your technique. You can do this through some forms of training or through honest evaluation of your own work to understand what works and what doesn't. The following approaches are listed in ascending order of likely cost.

## Review your previous work

The good news here is that this is the cheapest option to undertake. In addition, apart from cost, it will give you the greatest insight into what you might want to be working on. Look for the following areas for areas to enhance your photos:

### Technical issues

Did you have the right settings on the camera to produce the desired effect? This could include an aperture setting to give a pleasing depth of field, or a shutter speed that introduced just the right amount of blur to convey a sense of motion. Also, take the time to scan around the viewfinder to make sure that extraneous objects aren't protruding into the sides of the frame of the image. Trees, power lines, random body parts of strangers – these are all the culprits that turn up unexpectedly in the periphery of a frame. It pays to quickly scan the frame before pressing the shutter button.

### Story

Can a viewer look at the photo and understand the story that you were hoping to convey? If you were asked to pick your favourite photo taken that day, would this be that photo? If not, why not?

<u>Timing</u>

Perhaps everything in the photo came together from a logistical standpoint, however the light just wasn't on your side. This is the reality of travel photography, and so the lesson here could simply be to plan your next visit to a location at a time of day / time of year with a greater chance of decent light.

> **Tip:** Identify 1-2 areas for improvement to focus on or assess yourself on during the trip. If you attempt to remember to do 27 things differently, chances are that you'll get none of them right! This is a sure recipe for disaster and a miserable time. And probably not many decent photos.

# Self-study

Similar to reading this guide, there are many great books and videos that help explain topics such as how to use your specific camera, composition considerations, and storytelling. The latter tends to be the most overlooked study area, as most people often get stuck into the technical elements of taking a photo.

A great place to draw inspiration about effective storytelling is to view paintings. In this medium, the artist has plenty of time to compose an image that conveys exactly the elements that they want to help tell a story. This gives you some ideas on how subjects interact with each other in an image.

# Online training

The sheer quantity of online training available is astounding these days. This can run the range from free YouTube videos focusing on a particular technique / travel photography sub-genre, through to online webinars and training courses that seek to run you from soup to nuts in how to be a travel photographer.

Often price may not be the best way to determine whether the content is of any value; instead focus on user reviews. When reading negative reviews, do bear in mind that people learn in different ways and the training may simply have not resonated with a person through no real fault of the training material.

It can become very seductive to continuously watch YouTube videos and take training courses in the vain hope that this alone will transform your work. The reality is that you will need to put in effort yourself, and it might pay to pause videos and practice as you go.

> **Tip:** As above, watching / completing training is not a direct substitute for practice. Taking photos is almost costless (wear and tear will eventually affect your camera) and so trial and error is the best way to supplement any training.

# Workshops / classes

Possibly the best way to turbo-charge your learning, make sure that you seek out workshops and classes that will give you specific feedback on your technique and compositions. A good workshop or class (and to an extent, walking photo tour) will provide a greater return on investment by helping point out the specific areas that you need to be focusing on for your personal development.

In the round, this means that the upfront cost should save you a lot of time and effort, and frustration. When costed out, compared with online training (that isn't personalised) and hours of time invested, the cost of a workshop or class is more than likely going to come out cheaper in the longer run.

**Tip:** Where possible, approach a workshop / class with your known development areas already in mind. Seek feedback from the teacher as soon as possible on these areas, as this could further enhance your learning as you niche down on what is going to be most important for you.

# ADMINISTRATIVE MATTERS

Let's be honest, administrative tasks can often range from being an annoyance to the bane of one's existence. We love the notion of freedom associated with travel, however when you're visiting somebody else's land, you have to play on their terms. Depending on the purpose of your travel, duration, and what passport(s) you hold, this may or may not be trivial to resolve. Some of the ideas below apply to all travel, although visas don't come into play for domestic travel.

## VISAS AND CUSTOMS

For the purposes of this guide, we are going to work on the assumption that the activities that you plan to undertake in a location are considered acceptable under the rules and restrictions of a tourist visa of the country that you are visiting. Taking photos (or video) are acceptable as normal activities in this day and age, and even expensive equipment should no cause immigration / customs officers to bat an eyelid. There are a few things to consider to in avoiding delays / disappoints / confiscations:

### Visa vs visa -waiver

As a rule, check in advance to see whether you require a visa or visa-waiver in advance to visit a country (page 120). The situation changes fairly fluidly, and what was once a simplistic visa / visa-waiver on arrival now requires a little forward planning. Countries like the United States, Canada, Australia, and New Zealand operate a visa-waver program that requires a nominal fee and a small amount of information submitted in advance of your flight. The duration of validity will vary by country.

> **Tip:** Make sure you have at least six months validity left in your passport for the dates that you travel. The actual requirement for some countries can be less than six months, however this gives you a margin of time and avoids any complications.

### Tourism vs working

Tourism means that you will not be working, in particular, not taking up a job that a local could be performing. This means that if you are being hired to shoot an event or portrait, this may constitute work and therefore fall outside of the scope of a tourist visa. The likelihood of you being tripped up by this varies from country to country, and you may be able to get a simple business visa instead. Basic business visas that exist in the same realm as tourist visas for many countries cover activities such as attending conferences, meetings with local offices, etc. If in doubt, consult the embassy of the country that you are visiting.

# Customs declarations

If you have lots of shiny camera equipment and you are questioned by a customs official on arrival, you may need to explain that you're taking photos as a hobby (assuming this to be the case) and that you will be returning home in however many days (be prepared to show return flights if needed). They may also require you to "bond" your equipment on a form and declare that you'll be taking the equipment out of the country at the end of your stay. There is no harm in doing this as you intend to leave with all of your stuff anyway!

# A specific note about drones

Some countries outright ban the use of drones for security and / or privacy reasons, and so will confiscate any drones that are detected upon entry to the country. Usually this means that you will be able to collect the drone when you depart, however plan in advance and don't get caught out leaving your expensive toy in the hands of others. At the time of writing, India is a country that will confiscate your drone if detected on entry (all bags are scanned during customs), and you won't be getting it back!

# TRAVEL INSURANCE

Nobody thinks that they need travel insurance until they do. There are a variety of types of coverage out there, although pay close attention to the following as they are more relevant to travel photographers than the average traveller:

# Stolen / lost equipment cost

It is unlikely that you'll be able to get coverage for all of your equipment with a standard travel policy. You can consider taking the risk, approach the insurer for custom coverage, or seek out specific professional insurance for photographers. Or just leave some of the equipment at home!

# Trip duration

Most policies have a limit on the number of days per trip, ranging from 30, 45, or even up to 90 days. If you are planning on taking a longer trip than this, search online for insurance that is aimed at "nomads" or "digital nomads".

# Location coverage

Make sure that your travel insurance covers all countries that you are visiting, even those that you are only transiting through. Even if you are not planning on visiting the United States but happen to be transiting through, you will have to technically enter the country.

This has an implication on both arranging a visa (or ESTA visa waiver if eligible) as well as potential insurance coverage.

## Altitude

Make sure you check the insurance policy terms to determine the maximum altitude you will be covered for. Usually, standard travel insurance will specifically exclude anything that could remotely be construed as mountain climbing. If your intent is to visit Everest Base Camp to get some amazing photos as part of your Nepal trip, or you're heading to somewhere less ambitious yet at a high altitude, make sure that you are covered.

## Medical costs coverage

While the immediate hospitalisation costs may not be overbearing, you could sadly end up with a long rehabilitation process which could financially wipe you out if not covered. In addition, a medical evacuation back to your home country will become an expensive proposition very quickly, including airfares (which will likely be in a premium travel class) as well as accompanying medical staff (who will also be sitting next to you, in that premium travel class), and getting to and from airports.

# VACCINATIONS

There are places in the world that you may travel to where the risk of infectious diseases rises dramatically. This can range from the likes of cholera and typhoid, which can be vaccinated against, through to Sexually Transmitted Infections (STIs) or infections such as hepatitis. We have discussed this in greater detail later on (page 140).

Some vaccinations can be a multi-stage process, such as Hepatitis A or B. This means planning your vaccination regime well in advance of travel, potentially up to six months ahead. Consult your doctor for further information.

# MEDICATION AND SUPPLEMENTS

As we get older, or sick / injured, medication simply becomes a facet of life. Thrown into this mix can be a combination of supplements that we've incorporated into our diet in an effort to maintain peak physical health. Some things to bear in mind when traveling with medication:

# Prescription medication

The level of control over drugs will vary from country to country, sometimes even between territories of the same country. If you are taking medication that helps with pain management (as an example), this needs to be both clearly labelled with your name. Also ensure that you are carrying an amount that is appropriate for personal consumption only. If in doubt, consult your doctor for further information, and carry the prescription with you as further proof of your eligibility to take the drug(s).

# Carrying your medication

Using a pill box can reduce the amount of space required for medication, as well as help you keep track of what day it is when on holiday!

**Tip:** Make sure that you carry several days' worth of essential medication in your carry-on bag when flying, if not all of it. At very least this should cover you in case of delay or being stranded somewhere.

# Altitude sickness

Medication used to combat altitude sickness, such as Diamox, are often restricted from sale over the counter at a pharmacy. Make sure that you allow sufficient time to obtain a prescription and get that prescription filled before your travel.

# Pill form vs liquid form medication

If you use supplements in a liquid form, investigate whether it is possible to switch to a pill or powder form. This reduces weight, enables ease of carrying medication in your carry-on baggage for a flight, and reduces the risk of a mess in your bag of a liquid container breaking during transit.

# COPIES OF TRAVEL DOCUMENTS / KEY INFORMATION

Having your key travel documents and bookings readily available isn't always as straightforward as pulling out your smartphone. The dreaded flat phone battery can mean the difference between relaxing at the airport bar versus explaining to increasingly exasperated airport security staff that you do indeed have a plane ticket to fly home in an hour!

If you are traveling with multiple electronic devices such as smartphones, tablets, and laptops, aim to have your key documents saved on each of the devices where possible. If you're traveling as light as possible, then paper printouts don't weigh much and pack down into compact size and can be discarded when no longer needed.

Having physical printouts can also be helpful in specific situations, in addition to the above nightmare scenario:

- The printout of the hotel booking can easily be handed to a taxi driver or hotel clerk without fear of them somehow running off with your phone.
- Asking for directions of others, when you don't speak the language of the destination, is much easier when you have a printout of the address in the local language, or a map of your destination.
- In case you delete the email with your booking!

The documents that makes the most sense to have electronic copies of include the items below:

- Photo page of your passport
- Driver license
- Credit card (and CVV number) - this allows you to make online bookings even if you can't find the card
- Visas

Using a password management system such as LastPass or 1Password safely encrypts your data to minimise the chance of it being stolen by hackers

Make sure that you've retained electronic copies of the following, either by saving the original files (e.g. PDF / email) or emailing the data to yourself:

- Flights
- Hotel bookings
- Key activity bookings

# PHOTOGRAPHY PERMITS

In order to take photographs in certain locations, you may require advance permission. This is particularly true if you plan to take photos in some parks, or inside some buildings, museums, or monuments. Typically, if your photos are going to be used for private purposes, there doesn't tend to be any restriction. However, if you plan on selling the photos, even as Editorial (page 90), you may require permission.

Many places can even impose restrictions on your ability to share any photos on social media (Instagram, Facebook, YouTube, etc), although the chances of you getting into trouble are pretty minimal unless you're a huge social media star. At worst, the venue management could issue you with a "take down" notice to remove the offending image(s), which isn't the end of the world.

like most other matters covered in this administrative section, the earlier that you start the process for arranging permission, the greater the chances of successfully having the right permits for when you arrive.

**Tip:** Sometimes the mere act of having to get permission to photograph something will be your opportunity to visit a place that few other tourists get to see. As the permit becomes a "barrier to entry", it deters all but the most committed, and so you can count yourself amongst the few that have made the effort and therefore enjoy the spoils!

# MAKING BOOKINGS

Starting to put your plan in place can sometimes feel stressful, or it can help to build the anticipation of your trip. The earlier you start nailing down the core elements of your plan, such as transport and accommodation, the easier the rest of the trip planning will feel.

# ADVANCE BOOKING OF ACTIVITIES / ENTRIES

Getting some of the key bookings for your trip booked in advance means that you will not have to worry about sorting tickets out when on the ground, and potentially you can save money in the process. Here are some advance bookings that you may want to resolve before your trip:

## Making sure that the photo opportunity(s) exists

If the purpose of your trip is to visit specific locations, or attend particular events, make sure that these get confirmed very early in the booking process. Arriving at your destination to find out that the tickets to the venue have sold out, or that the museum is closed for renovation can put a dampener on your mood. Or worse, the monument you want to photograph is currently undergoing renovation / restoration and is enveloped in scaffolding – this happens quite often!

## "Skip the line" tickets

When time is of the essence, the queue is long, your feet are tired, and the sun is beating down on those in line, you'll be very glad that you paid the extra money for a "skip the line" type entry. Skip the line type tickets can feel like they add to your trip cost, and cumulatively can add up. However, consider the time saving gained in each instance. For example, for an extra \$5 / €5 / ¥100, you will save yourself 30 minutes of standing around. This frees up your time for other things, and leaves you feeling less tired / stressed. That's often a good exchange for the money.

## Cheaper prices

As a general rule, the further ahead in time that you book the trip, the cheaper the cost is likely to be. This is principally because there are greater options available, including cheaper fares that get snapped up quicker. It is also because the vendor is wanting to offer a discount for making a commitment so far in advance. As a rule, booking at least three weeks in advance can give you great savings with a reasonable choice. For holiday periods, including Christmas / New Year (globally), expect to pay over the odds no matter how far in advance

ou book. It's simple economics, where the demand well outstrips the supply, and sellers are
more than happy to capitalise on this.

# HOTELS AND OTHER ACCOMMODATION

Here are some considerations for booking accommodation that may help contribute to your
photo opportunities during your trip.

## Booking a room with a view

Imagine being able to wake up in the morning, open the shutters, and look out onto an
Italian piazza, or the mountains, or sea. Many hotels advertise rooms with "city view" or
"seaside view" etc. however, there can sometimes need to be a bit of expectation
management. There are few things that you can do to improve your odds of getting a decent
room:

### Google Maps Street View (or equivalent)

Use this tool to "virtually" walk around the hotel. When you "look up", check to see if you
get a sense that the windows of this hotel will actually face onto the scene that is in your
mind?

### Online reviews

Have a look at hotel booking websites, as well as blogs. Sometimes the view is mentioned,
particularly if it is of significance.

### Call / email the hotel

Be open and honest about what you are looking for, and ideally see if the hotel can send you
photos of the view from the room, and let you know which room(s) will have that view.
Make sure that your booking clearly states that you've booked Room x (the one with the
view shown).

### Room with no view

This can come in several forms, from a view of the drainpipes in the small ventilation shaft
in the middle of the building, to the inner courtyard just facing other rooms of the hotel.
The worst can be the hotel room with no windows (we're not counting capsule hotels here!).

Often the hotel disguises or hides the fact that the room has no windows, and it's only when
you look at the fine print detail of the room details that this becomes apparent. Usually these
rooms are significantly cheaper than other rooms at the hotel, which can often be the tip-off

to look further into this. Worst case, the hotel might have a good roof terrace!

## Roof terrace / bar / restaurant

This can often turn out to be better than the room itself for a few reasons. Often there isn't a pane of glass between you and what you are looking to photograph. There also can be 360 degrees views, opening up more photographic opportunities. And, you can potentially enjoy a drink while you capture sunset shots!

## Expensive views

What if the hotel has a view that is killer, yet charges an arm and a leg for the privilege? Perhaps you are able to access this view from an associated roof terrace that the public can access, even if it means buying a drink? An expensive cocktail is still cheaper than a night in the hotel!

Alternatively, consider staying in the hotel for one night simply to get the vantage points that you want, and stay somewhere that is more within your budget for the remainder of the time. Ideally look to stay in the room with the killer view at the very start or end of your trip to reduce logistical hassles from moving from one hotel to another. Just be aware that there is a risk that there could be bad weather during your stay. Like every part of your trip, timing and good luck with the weather are key.

## International travel

Make sure that you have at least your first night of accommodation booked when traveling to an international destination. Most countries will require an address on an immigration form. So long as you know where you'll be on the first night, you'll have something to write down. Not having a place to stay is likely to invite a lengthy conversation with the immigration officer, and this will get your trip off to a bad start.

# Private property stays

This can come in three main forms, each of which has its pros and cons as it relates to a photo trip:

## Friends and family

This can be a fantastic opportunity to catch with the long-lost cousin, or the friend that you haven't seen in a while. There's also a good chance that the accommodation and food during your stay won't cost anything, too. What's not to like here?!?

Well… Consider that the best times of the day to take photos are often fairly unsocial hours and / or conflict with mealtimes. If you can agree in advance with your hosts that you will be out and about during certain times, this can avoid disappointment or embarrassment once you are their guest. Your hosts may (reasonably) expect you to be spending time with them, eating dinner with them, sleeping in bed at dawn like the rest of the population.

our best bet is to chat with your host in advance and see if this can work. Or, you could consider a hybrid option of staying with them for part of your trip, and alternative accommodation for the rest of the time. Also note that couch surfing and other "staying with strangers" variants come with the same perks and pitfalls.

## Private property stay marketplaces (such as AirBnB)

This is definitely an option that should be explored, particularly if your stay is going to be more than a few days. The costs often are cheaper than hotels, you'll get more space and privacy, cooking space, and a peek into what local housing is like. However, many cities / countries are clamping down on the use of such services as AirBnB and can even create legal issues for you if caught illegally using these services.

Logistically, finding your accommodation could prove a little more challenging, particularly if you arrive at night. If you are unsure about how to make this happen, consider a hybrid model of staying in a hotel for the first night, getting your bearings, and then obtaining the keys to the property at a leisurely hour with less stress.

## "Home stays" in traditional housing / communities

The concept here is simple; a home stay allows you to live like a local during your stay. Doing so will no doubt present you with excellent photo opportunities, not to mention getting insight into the local culture that no hotel could provide.

Bear in mind that this is an "experience" as much as anything else, and so should be thought of differently to a hotel. You are getting hospitality, and so will need to play your part in this, including being present for set mealtimes, engaging with your hosts, learning a little about them, and sharing experiences. And more often than not, being prepared to let them practice their English with you. A home stay should not be treated as an opportunity to have a quiet night or for when you're exhausted after days of running around a location!

# FLIGHTS

Whether you're an aviation geek (fascinated by planes / flying) or a nervous flyer, getting from A to B by plane can often be the most efficient (or only) way to get around.

## Working out where you want to fly to

This might feel like it is blindingly obvious, right? Let's say you are going to New York City (USA), or Krabi (Thailand), or Vienna (Austria). For each of these examples, there are alternative options that can be very appealing from a cost and logistical perspective. These alternatives also have the distinction of potentially better arrival times for flights, greater availability of flights, or paradoxically, can actually get you to your destination (hotel, conference, park, etc) quicker than the obvious airport option. To further illustrate the three examples above:

## Example one - multiple airports in a location

New York City (USA) - the two main airports serving NYC are John F. Kennedy airport (JFK) and La Guardia (LGA), both out to the East of Manhattan. JFK in particular takes at least an hour to get into Manhattan by taxi, car, bus, or subway (which is a hassle of itself). LGA is a bit more convenient, being on the North side of Queens, and you can usually get into Manhattan in around 30-45 minutes.

Now, consider the alternative option Newark (EWR), which is located across the Hudson river in New Jersey. You can get a train from Newark into New York Penn Station (not to be confused with New Jersey Penn Station!) in 27 minutes, or a bus to the New York Port Authority bus terminal (next to Times Square) in 45-60 minutes.

## Example two - a nearby airport

Krabi (Thailand) - this gorgeous beach and rock-climbing destination has an airport (KBV) located around 30 minutes from the beach resorts and areas that tourists congregate. However, if you fly into Phuket, suddenly a vast number of additional flight options are open to you, as Phuket is a much bigger airport and destination. Very affordable taxi transfers to Krabi can be booked at Phuket airport itself (or in advance), and a comfortable two-hour ride later you'll arrive at your destination on a beach in Krabi.

## Example three - a nearby airport in a different country

Vienna (Austria) - the Austrian capital has its own airport (VIE), which takes you 16 minute by train to get into the city centre. Some airlines, particularly low-cost European airlines, advertise "Vienna" and actually fly into Bratislava airport (BTS) in neighbouring European Union country Slovakia, with a transfer time into Vienna of 80 minutes by bus. If you don't require a visa to enter European Union countries (or have a Schengen visa), this alternative option could be a boon for you as flights into Vienna can often be more expensive.

The above three examples are to promote the idea of thinking more laterally about what travel options suit you best. So, how can you discover these alternate routes? A great place to start is by looking at a map of the area, and search for nearby airports.

Each airport will have its IATA three-digit code, which can be plugged into flight aggregators or airline websites (both described below). Some of the better aggregators will also give you a "search nearby" option to expand the number of potential airports that you can fly into.

# Stopovers

A stopover (or layover) can come about for a few different reasons, sometimes without you having any choice in the matter. For example, there are no direct flights between your departure and destination locations. Quite often this can be because the airline you've chosen has a hub location somewhere between where you're starting and finishing, or that your start and / or end locations are lower-trafficked and therefore less flight options. A stopover could even be as simple as a "direct" service which means that it can stop in an airport (or more) along your route. Only "non-stop" flights go from A to B with no stopovers; a nuance that most people outside of the airline industry are not aware of.

A stopover can be as simple as having to sit in your seat while the departing passengers get off and new passengers board, which is much more likely for domestic flights. More often in these situations, all passengers will be required to disembark the plane and re-board when the plane is ready to depart for its next destination (usually due to safety when refuelling). Alternatively, a stopover can be a long wait in an airport departure lounge before your next flight.

If you are flying internationally, several national carriers advertise flight options that include stopovers in their country, including a simplistic tourist visa if you'd like to spend the day exploring a new city. This can be a fantastic way to expand your itinerary to take in another city, relieve boredom of the airport and stretch your legs. You could even have accommodation included in the deal, so you'll have a chance to shower and get some sleep! To get these types of fares, you'll usually need to book your flights through the airline's website.

Check out the section (page 125) on countries that have stopover tourist visas.

# Flight aggregators

Similar to other aggregators, flight aggregators (page 118) are an indispensable resource for finding the best flight opportunities for your trip, including best departure and / or arrival times, cost, and airline or airline group (One World, Star Alliance, Sky Team, etc). For straightforward travel arrangements, these are the best place to start, even if you're loyal to one airline (or airline group). The points below can also apply to travel agents.

The downsides to these services can include the following challenges:

## Open-jaw tickets

This expression relates to a trip that involves flying into one airport, and flying home from another. An example of this could be a trip to London (United Kingdom) that arrives at London Heathrow (LHR) and then departs from London Gatwick (LGW). In this specific example, you can search for the IATA area term "LON" which includes all six London airports (Heathrow, Gatwick, Stansted, City, Luton, and Southend-on-Sea), however other smaller locations don't have the same option.

## Frequent-flyer (FF) points maximisation is difficult

For those readers that are always looking for the best way to get the most frequent flyer points, this section is probably re-capping the basics. For the rest of us, something to bear in mind is that aggregators typically optimise their flight options that are displayed based on price or departure / arrival time, and not more nuanced concepts such as FF points earned.

## Checked baggage allowances

It can sometimes be difficult to determine whether a flight sold through an aggregator includes checked baggage, and what that checked baggage allowance may be. This is particularly true with low-cost airlines that charge for every element of the flight experience.

## "Fly-by-night" aggregators

If the price is "too good to be true", then chances are that the flight price is too good to be true! Stick to the major aggregators to avoid disappointment. Another challenge is that some smaller aggregators will claim that they've secured the ticket at a certain price, and then several days later come back and inform you that the flight ticket had been sold out at that price point or that the flight is fully booked. They will then take their time in refunding your money. Meanwhile, you've lost time in finding the right fare, and you're back at square one again. And then potentially having to chase the aggregator for your refund.

## Changes to bookings

If you need to cancel a flight, or change flight timing, aggregators can introduce change costs over and above what the airline charges for changes or make it impossible to make a change. Alternatively, if you have extenuating circumstances for a need to change (e.g. bout of adult chicken pox, broken limb, etc), airlines can often be sympathetic to your plight and arrange a change for what was otherwise a "non-refundable" fare. Aggregators, not so much…

## When things go wrong

Flight delay and / or cancellation is statistically inevitable the more often that you travel. Depending on where you are, this can range from a small inconvenience, to potentially large costs involved in getting to or from your destination. As a rule-of-thumb, you get what you pay for with airline service – the more you pay (including class of travel), the better the service should be.

One challenge that many flyers encounter with flights purchased through aggregators is that the airline customer service can try to push you back to the aggregator to get help / support when things go wrong. And similar to the airline "get what you pay for" concept, aggregators can vary in the level of service that you can expect in such situations.

Having read all of the above points, you may be wondering why even bother with aggregators?! The reality is that most of the time, for straightforward travel that goes to plan (which is the majority of the time), there are no hiccups. Aggregators will allow you to save yourself a bit of money, and you will be able to shop for the best option that suits your travel needs.

You may want to use an airline's website directly if you're flying at a time when there is a higher than average likelihood of flight disruption, such as:

- Wintertime across the United States and Canada (particularly the East coast), the United Kingdom, and Northern Europe, when snow can be forecast or expected.
- Best weather periods for different countries (page 136).

# Reward flights

A reward ticket is one purchased using Frequent Flyer (FF) points, or other similar means. A whole book can be written on this topic, including effective strategies for collecting, using, and transferring points between programs. Some suggested resources are included in the reference section of this guide (page 118).

# Checked baggage

If you decide that you need to travel with checked baggage, or that you need to purchase additional baggage beyond your existing allowance, make sure you add this to your itinerary before checking-in online, or before you get to the airport. Airlines love to charge a premium for last-minute decisions, and your checked baggage allowances can (usually) be anticipated ahead of time. A suggestion for flights where you're required to choose between checked baggage weights, opt for the size that is the next one up from what you think you need (e.g. 20kg instead of 15kg).

> **Tip:** Paying a little extra money avoids the stress of packing to keep your weight just within the limit.

# TRAINS

Before there were planes, there were trains. The quality and pervasiveness of train travel varies from country to country and can sometimes be perceived as an inferior alternative to travel by plane.

Many countries are easily navigable by train, and in fact it's often the preferred method for most countries across Europe. With the exception of the Eastern seaboard, the United States is one stand-out country that trains are not going to be the most effective way to get around. Consider the following benefits of travel by train:

## Cost

Particularly when purchased in advance, long distance train travel can often be cheaper than flights alone. This is typically due to country norms, where most people will travel by train between locations hence greater economies of scale. Refer to national rail carrier section (page 120) for their websites.

## Central stations are, well, central

The invention of the steam train, and the opportunities that rail travel provided, meant that major train stations often had a very central (and visible) position within most cities, where they remain to today. You will arrive at your destination right in the thick of it all, with no concerns about peak hour traffic etc. preventing you reaching (getting to the hotel is a separate matter).

On the flipside, airports are largely positioned to be away from urban centres, and often can be a bit of a trek to reach. This adds to your journey time at both the departure and arrival ends of your journey. Also, it can often be an hour or more on either side of your flight.

## End-to-end journey time

Building on the point above about getting to and from airports, another time factor that needs to be considered for flying is the amount of time taken to get through airport security and to then board the plane. At your destination, you will have to get off the plane, traverse the airport terminal, collect baggage etc. This can usually add a minimum one hour to the departure time, and 30 minutes to the arrival time.

## (Mostly) lack of security screening

For the majority of train journeys, you do not have to go through any security screening process. There are exceptions to this such as Eurostar travel between the United Kingdom, France, and Belgium, as well as long distance train travel in Spain. However, the screening process is often much less restrictive than airlines, including no issues related to carrying liquids. This means you can stock up on food and drinks before you board the train and enjoy a picnic in your seat as you travel to your destination.

## Less baggage restrictions

If you are traveling with one or two bags, nobody is waiting to weigh them before you get onto the train. The only restriction, as such, is actually how many bags can you herd across a platform and lug onto the train. Most long-distance trains will have storage areas in each carriage to leave your larger bags, and theft is unlikely to be a concern, particularly if your train doesn't stop between where you board and your destination. You can always sit where you can see your bags if you're concerned.

## View out of the window

Perhaps the most overlooked advantage of train travel is the ability to get a sense for both the country and changing landscapes. Whilst photos of the landscape outside of the window requires a very fast shutter speed, and preferably good light, simply watching the world go by is part of the journey. Enjoy it!

**Tip:** When taking photos of objects outside of the train, make sure that the window itself is clean (the higher up the window, the greater the chance of cleanliness). Set your camera to Shutter priority or a high shutter speed to avoid capturing a blurry mess. The unique perspective that you'll get of near objects being blurry and static (or near static) distant objects will immediately signal to your viewer that it is a travel photo.

## Moving about in the cabin

Seat belts aren't a concept that applies to trains, and there are not going to be restrictions on when you can move about in the train. This is particularly good news for taller people who can avoid discomfort and potentially stand for extended periods of time. Longer journeys can even include a bar or a restaurant carriage, and you can stand or sit and enjoy some food or drinks at your pace.

## No turbulence

For those who aren't exactly fond of flying, including those who suffer from a fear of heights, the train can be the ideal solution for you. Not only do you stay close to the ground, being able to see out the windows and fix your gaze on objects in the distance can help calm any fears that may arise.

# TRANSFERS

A transfer is the means by which you get from your main mode of transport (usually a plane) to your destination (such as a hotel). Transfers can range from a shuttle bus, to a taxi, or even a boat (e.g. Venice). Many hotels offer free airport transfers as part of their accommodation package, and so make sure you get in touch with the hotel in advance to take advantage of this service.

Even if there is no transfer included in your hotel booking, consider booking one in advance for the following scenarios:

## Unfamiliar places

If you are visiting a place for the first time and are unsure of how to get from A to B, a transfer booked in advance can remove the majority of this stress for you. Sometimes, the incremental cost of arranging a transfer in advance can be minimal compared to on-the-spot prices. This holds true for places where you do not speak the local language, and English is unlikely to be pervasive.

## Difficult to find locations

It is reasonable to believe that all physical address systems work the same around the world. The variances from country to country include the notation for describing what floor a place is on (this may not be so apparent for many Asian countries), buildings aren't even numbered, or having a numbering system that is hard to understand for Western tourists (e.g. Japan's numbering based on blocks rather than streets).

## Arriving in the dark

Darkness adds to the perceptual challenge of sorting yourself out getting to your destination. The actual risk may be substantially lower than the perceived risk in the evening or night.

## Arriving after an overnight flight

There's a fair chance that your brain is pretty much mush after a long-haul flight, particularly if it's been a pretty uncomfortable overnight sleep in Economy class. In addition to the small bit of luxury it provides, a transfer booked in advance takes the guesswork out of navigating a transport system that you may not be familiar with.

## You've got bags

This may be stating the obvious, however the more bags you add to the mix, the more effort required and the more frustration that can be induced trying to get them from the airport to your accommodation.

# CARS / BIKES

Going on a trip to take photos by car opens up so many possibilities, particularly if you are able to assign driving responsibilities to somebody else! For some countries, attempting to drive requires fool's courage, nerves of steel, or both. In these places, and there are plenty of them, leave the driving to others (ideally locals) and focus on taking photos.

Some of the advantages of driving when weighing up the cost of car hire:

## Access

National parks, coastal areas, mountains, etc. typically aren't well served by public transport, if at all. Hiring a car, or hitch hiking, are your only options.

# Flexibility of timing

Imagine arriving at a beautiful location and discovering that your only bus / train / boat back to your hotel leaves in 30 minutes. This takes away from the ability to get the photos that you want, perhaps work a subject from different angles, or wait for better light. You'll always have one eye on the watch so that you don't get stranded. This of course doesn't apply to parking meters – those things are everywhere!

# Stopping by the side of the road

Being able to pull over if something catches your eye can add some unexpectedly interesting photos to your trip. You may even stumble across places or scenes that you had no idea about in your planning, and you'll have the good fortune to be able to take it in.

# Sunrises

In order to be in the perfect spot in time for sunrise, you will have to find a way to reach there. Sometimes this can mean leaving so that you arrive 30 minutes or more before sunrise to get a good position and to set up to be ready. Often capturing the morning light can take up to 1-2 hours if the conditions are great, at which point hunting around for the nearest taxi stand or bus stop may not be the most appealing option.

# Car (or bike) hire

If you are going to be hiring a car, there are several online resources that can help explain what to look out for when hiring a car. We'll focus here on the broader logistical considerations of driving in a foreign place. The same pointers generally apply to bikes.

## International driver's license

The need for international driver's licenses seems to vary from country to country although the international license itself may not be needed for car hire. Please bear in mind that just because you are able to hire a car with your existing license does not mean that you are therefore eligible to drive on the roads of that country. If in doubt, arrange for an international driver's license in advance (they usually last for 12 months), or contact the local police / road authority to confirm.

## Manual transmission cars

For those living in the United States, Canada, Australia, or New Zealand, automatic transmission cars have been the norm for a couple of decades now. However, for Europe and much of Asia, manual transmissions are still fitted to the majority of cars. This is partly due to higher fuel costs, smaller roads and cramped conditions necessitating smaller vehicles in general.

Petrol is much more expensive in these countries, and there has been a long-held perception that manual cars are more fuel-efficient. The relative benefits of this can be debated, however the point being that you are much more likely to end up with a manual transmission if you hire the car in Europe or Asia.

If this is going to be a challenge for you, make sure you specifically search out automatic cars. More premium model cars may also have a gear shift, so it pays to ask.

## Diesel cars

Europe leads the world with the uptake of diesel engine vehicles, accounting for around 50% of the cars on the road. It is important to know this, as petrol in diesel tanks can end up costing you a lot of money to get repaired.

Don't forget to ask when you collect the car from the hire car place. Ask the car hire place if the diesel car has a specific way that you need to start the engine (older diesels require the glow plugs to be warmed up first), although chances are nowadays that there isn't anything to worry about.

## Driving on the "wrong" side of the road

If you've never driven a left-hand drive car before, picking up a car from Los Angeles airport and making your way into gridlock traffic may not be your best introduction!

In such scenarios, consider a hybrid option of public transport or taxi to a less busy location to collect your car, and then return the car to the airport at the end of the trip. This means that when you start driving on the other side of the road, you're not competing with a large number of drivers. Leave that for day two.

# MAKING THE MOST OF YOUR TRIP

Now you get to bring all of the planning together and come away with the shots that you wanted. When taking a trip to principally take photos, if you think of it as an assignment, you are more likely to come away with what you are looking for. Treat it like work, and it can make you feel a little easier about getting up for an early sunrise, walking all day, and staying around to capture the sunset. A trip taking photos isn't a trip to the beach; you are more than likely going to be tired by the end of it. The following are ways that you can make the most of the trip, and hopefully enjoy yourself in the process.

# PACKING

Ensuring that you travel with everything that you need is a bit of an art as much as a science. Experience is generally the best way to help you work out what needs to come, and what can be left on the shelf at home for another time. Apart from being crucial to your photography trip, your cameras and lenses are often expensive pieces of equipment. They don't respond particularly well to being thrown about, and loss / theft of them will continue being a hassle long after your trip has finished.

Below are tips and suggestions on carrying your equipment, principally based around the idea that you're likely to be flying to and from your destination. The suggestions apply for other forms of transport, with car travel giving you the ability to be a little less strict about packing.

**Bonus:** Over the years, we have refined our packing lists to include everything required for different types of travel. We're providing a packing list that can be customised depending on the season, expected weather, and how much equipment you intend to carry.

Get your free packing list by heading over to
walkaboutphotoguides.com/travelphotosplanning/bonuses

# CARRY-ON BAGGAGE

On balance, traveling with less usually tends to be preferable to dragging along the kitchen sink and then not using it. Does this mean that you can get away with carry-on only? This will depend on your method of transport and how much space that you have.

Squeezing everything into a carry-on bag allows you to move seamlessly from one location to the next. Once you get off the train or plane, you can walk straight through to get a local train / bus / taxi to get to the next stop. However, airlines are usually very particular about the size and weight restrictions of carry-on baggage.

When up against the ever-changing landscape of what airlines will consider as carry-on baggage, here are some points of consideration:

- Generally speaking, "full service" airlines (e.g. national flag carrier airlines) tend to be more relaxed about baggage allowances, particularly for international flights. Conversely, budget airlines are notorious for their strictness on size and weight.
- Premium class passengers tend to have more flexible carry-on baggage allowances, as well as people with airline "status".
- Many airlines allow a piece of carry-on baggage as well as a small laptop bag / handbag (or purse). Typically, this second bag doesn't tend to get weighed, particularly handbags.
- Anything that you carry on your person is not subject to weight restriction. If your carry-on baggage is tipping the scales, put several of your heaviest items in your pockets. Items such as batteries, smaller lenses, even smaller camera bodies can slip into a pocket.
- Further to the point above, you can carry a jacket with pockets, that won't be subject to the weight restriction.
- Books are heavy, and you are usually allowed to carry reading material that isn't subject to the usual weight restrictions.

Whatever happens, do everything you can to avoid having to check-in a bag with your camera equipment as this is both expensive and fragile.

# CAMERAS, LENSES, AND OTHER ACCESSORIES

While this guide talks about what camera / lens combinations may be most effective for your travels, let's walk through some of the logistics of traveling with camera equipment with the following tips:

## Tripod

At the end of the end of the day, the best tripod is the one that travels with you and gets used. If you are going to be traveling light, or with carry-on baggage only, invest in a small and / or lightweight tripod to ensure that it's on hand for when you want to get that great long exposure shot.

# Lens blower

These little devices blow air in a targeted way when pinched, and so can be used to blow dust of camera sensors and lenses. When cleaning a DSLR sensor, make sure that you flip the mirror up (consult your DSLR's guide on this) and angle the camera downward so that the sensor is facing the ground. This means that any dirt that is blown off the sensor will fall down and out of the way.

# Lens cleaner

The glass on a lens can be surprisingly resilient however to protect your investment it is recommended that you use materials such as micro fibre cloth to give your lens a proper clean. They can be purchased cheaply, and you can amass a supply of them to carry in your camera bag at all times.

# Batteries

Running out of juice before you're finished taking photos can be a hugely frustrating experience! As can having to minimise your photo taking to optimise what little battery power you might have left. Make sure that you carry spare batteries for all key devices, including spares for camera flashes etc.

# Packing of batteries

When flying, you will need to ensure that all of your Lithium ion (Li-ion) batteries are carried in your carry-on baggage. There is a (very small) risk that these batteries can be damaged by changes in pressure which can start a fire. The idea is that if you carry the batteries in your carry-on baggage and it starts a blaze, you are much more likely to spot this during a flight. Planes carry a number of fire suppression options to deal with such instances, often without needing to affect the flight.

When checking-in at an airport, airlines are increasingly making this point that you can't have batteries in your checked baggage, so placing them in your carry-on avoids a discussion later on.

# ELECTRONICS (EXCLUDING CAMERAS)

This is usually where the bulk of the weight in your packed bag will come from (apart from your camera equipment!). Something that is becoming increasingly useful is to switch all of your devices to USB charging wherever possible. This will reduce the number of cables and plugs that you need to bring with you, allow you to borrow charging units from others, and allows you to take advantage of portable charger when in a pinch.

> **Tip:** Coiling up your electronic cables each time can reduce frustration and the need to untangle the cables. Picture trying to untangle that set of Christmas lights that were never packed away properly.

## Essentials

Don't leave home without these items:

- **Camera and lenses** - These will make your trip much more productive!

- **Phone charger cable** - This applies to any trip. Oh, and your phone.

- **USB charging hub** - Preferably buy a charger that outputs 2 Amp or more per socket to speed up the charging time per device.

- **Battery charger for camera** - Where possible, buy USB battery chargers for your camera batteries. This reduces weight and allows you to use a portable charger to charge the camera batteries when on the move.

- **Extra camera batteries** - This can't be stressed enough!

- **Memory cards** - Memory cards are so cheap these days, there isn't really an excuse for not having enough of them with you to shoot. Make sure that the existing data on the memory cards has been backed up and then format the cards before your trip.

- **Travel adapter** - If you find yourself traveling to the same destination repeatedly (and still need a travel adapter), consider using specific plug converters rather than universal travel adapters. These are going to be cheaper, smaller, lighter, and less hassle to plug into power points.

- **Portable charger for USB devices** - This can help bring life back into your phone, or charge camera batteries during the day if you don't have many (or any) spares.

## Good to have items

These items will make your life a little easier, however they do come with drawbacks such as weight, ability to insure, necessity:

- **Power strip / power board** - This is useful when traveling to a destination that uses a different power plug, as you can use one adapter for several devices.

- **External hard disk** - Being able to back up your photos onto multiple locations when on the move is very important. Don't carry external hard disks that require separate power (these are less common these days). When purchasing an external hard disk, spending the extra few dollars / pounds on a ruggedized enclosure can provide a little extra piece of mind.

- **Laptop / tablet device -** Depending on your weight and space restrictions, these give you many more options for reviewing your photos as you travel. They also are pretty handy for doing some preliminary culling of photos and edits during the hours when you stuck on a plane / train!

- **USB memory stick -** These little devices are great for backing up when on the go, and for carrying a copy of all of the images from your trip in your pocket.

# ACCESSORIES

Many of the items here are subjective and can be dependent on where you're traveling:

## Sun cream

If in doubt, wear sun cream (also known as sun screen) when heading out. Ideally SPF 50 (or greater), however any sun cream is better than none. The following situations tend to increase the likelihood of getting sun burnt:

- Altitude - Higher altitudes come with an innate higher risk of getting burnt.
- Hot weather - The big yellow circle in the sky comes with some nasty side effects.
- Snow - In addition to the direct rays coming down, reflected sun rays off the snow can lead to burning of areas not normally affected (e.g. under the nose).
- Water - As per snow (above).
- Overcast days - This can often be the most deceptive time, as the sun isn't directly beaming down on you.

## Medication / supplements

If traveling for a shorter trip, consider using a pill box to reduce the amount of space required if carrying lots of medication. Carrying a small supply of anti-diarrheic (e.g. Imodium), antihistamines (e.g. Clarityn), and paracetamol can also come in handy. Refer to the section on first aid for further suggestions (page 145).

## Umbrella

The object that you never want to use on a travel photography trip because it means one hand is now out of action (holding the umbrella). In addition, photographing rainy conditions can be both dreary and risk damaging your equipment. On the plus side, an umbrella can also be used to avoid the harsh sun, something that is very common to see in

Asian countries.

## Toiletries

Notwithstanding the requirements around liquids in major airports, look to minimise your toiletries in a few ways to help reduce your overall luggage. Roll-on / stick deodorant is more robust for the rigours of travel. Look for small tubes of toothpaste for sale, or simply save your half-finished toothpaste to specifically use when traveling.

## Toilet paper

Depending on where you're traveling to, this can be a life saver! Many public facilities may not have toilet paper, and you don't want to get caught short! In a pinch, toilet paper can also be used to clean surfaces, as well as your hands.

# CLOTHING

If you are reading this guide, chances are that you're planning trips to take photos. You are willing to let your fashionista ways take a back seat to practicality, at least for this trip! Many of the items below may feel blindingly obvious, however preparedness can be key to a successful trip:

## Shoes

Possibly the most important item of clothing that you're taking. This is not the time to break in new shoes. Comfort is the name of the game, so make sure that you wear-in any new shoes at home before they are needed. If in doubt, carry plasters and apply them to your feet BEFORE you head out and about.

If you are traveling to a location that is likely to require you to be taking your shoes off several times a day (visiting temples, holy places, indoor locations, etc), having shoes that are easy to take off and tie up is a huge bonus.

## Socks

If you are going to be walking for hours on end, try wearing compression socks (or ski socks) to help with blood flow and reduce fatigue. It is possible to get ankle-length compression socks as well, to give your feet a little extra support.

## Pants

For warmer months of the year, having pants that unzip as shorts are a versatile way to dress. Many places of worship will have dress codes, and it's respectful to abide by these. Covering your extremities is made easier with zip-off legs, as the bottom sections can be easily reapplied before going inside.

## Shirts / tops

Similar to the point above, long-sleeved shirts can be rolled down when entering places that require conservative dress. Long-sleeved shirts can also help if the sun is incredibly strong and risk of sun burn is very high. Collared shirts are also more comfortable if you're wearing a neck strap for your camera.

## Hat / head covering

Protection from the sun is important in hot weather, particularly for those with shorter (or no) hair on top. It helps prevent sun burn, as well as providing a degree of shade for your face and neck.

## Jacket / sweater

When looking at the weather forecast for a destination, pay particular attention to the overnight temperatures. If in doubt, take a light jacket which can be layered with shirts if required, to keep you warm at night.

# PACKING EFFICIENTLY

Packing efficiently is an art form in itself, although the following are some tips that can help you out:

## Packing lists

Creating a packing list several days before you actually need to leave means that you will be able to keep adding to the list as you think of more items. Keep these packing lists, as they can often be reused for future journeys.

## Weight distribution

If you know that there is a chance that you'll be lugging your bags at any point during your journey, do your best to place the most weight possible at the lowest point of the bag. For wheeled bags this means over the wheels, and for backpacks this should be around the waist area. This will make it easiest to manoeuvre your bags through crowded airports, train stations, taxi stands, busy streets etc.

## Plastic bags

The huge versatility and almost zero weight of plastic bags means that you should always carry a few in your bags for all sorts of scenarios. If you have dirty, particularly wet, clothing or shoes that need to be packed, you can avoid contaminating the rest of your bag. If you need to keep all of your small cables and electronic odds-and-ends in one place, reach for a plastic bag. A plastic bag can also be used as an impromptu water protector for your camera if you're out shooting in wet conditions.

## Dry sacks

On those occasions when an umbrella just isn't going to cut it, a dry sack can ensure that you avoid a soaked mobile phone or soggy passport, and the associated tears that come with this! Dry sacks can be purchased in different sizes, including those big enough for just your wallet, passport, and phone. If you are caught short, zip lock bags can be a cheap substitute, however it can sometimes not provide as convincing a seal.

> **Tip:** Most things can be purchased at your destination. Don't feel the need to bring the kitchen sink, or duplicates of all of your electronic cables, just in case!

> **Advanced tip:** If you travel frequently, even if not for photography, invest in a separate set of the following. These can live permanently in your travel bag, and only used for travel:
>
> - Toiletries including stick / roll-on deodorant, sun cream, and toothpaste / toothbrush combo.
> - Electronic cables for charging key devices such as your phone and laptop.
> - Hats, particularly those that fold down easily for packing.

# MONEY

The topic of handling your money when traveling is somewhat personal to your circumstances, and the location that you're visiting. There are still a variety of places that run on cash / coins (e.g. Japan), or places that may not accept the forms of credit card that you have. The intricacies are too complex to cover in this guide. Here are some general tips that re somewhat universal:

# Carrying local currency

If you are used to a world of paying for everything with plastic or contactless, a return to handling cash may feel like a step into the past! Coupled with the feeling of nostalgia is getting to grips with a foreign currency (especially for the first time) which adds one more dimension to your trip. There are advantages to using cash, as described below:

## Don't get caught short

Your chances of being unable to pay with cash are slim to none in most parts of the world. Plus, you don't have to go through the whole 'card machine is broken' conversational dance, including wondering whether they're telling you the truth or not!

## Speed

Cash is quick! Unless you're trying to break large notes, in which case you need to be a little strategic about it (page 59).

## No card fraud risk

By paying with cash, there is no risk that somebody is "skimming" your card during the transaction to later commit credit card fraud.

## Immersion

Handling cash like a local is one more way that you are blending in and becoming ever so slightly less of a tourist. In addition, understanding the challenges of working with another currency can give you better insight into how locals think about their money.

To illustrate this, in Indonesia the Indonesian Rupiah currency is approximately 14,000 to the US dollar (February 2019, subject to massive fluctuation!). Locals in many venues will list the prices omitting the one thousand unit, whereby 25,000 is shown as 25 (or 25k). This has a psychological impact in feeling that prices are potentially cheaper.

## Use "clean" notes

Retailers and banks in many countries will reject notes that contain tears (or missing edges) or have pen / marker scribbled on them. You can refuse to take certain notes if you feel that they aren't in good shape, and here a small degree of tact or diplomacy goes a long way!

## Watch out for the "no change" vendor

This infuriating scenario can vary from general unhelpfulness through to outright scam. When changing notes, ask for smaller denominations wherever possible. If you happen to have large denomination notes, try to exchange them in your hotel or when at a larger restaurant / shop.

> **Tip:** If the amount of change that you're expecting isn't a big amount in your local currency, consider writing off the amount as a donation / gift. Whilst the "principle" of being short-changed sucks, the relative cost and value of the currency for you versus the vendor may ultimately make you feel petty about quibbling about the cost.
>
> Consider it good karma!

## Avoiding counterfeit currency

Identifying counterfeit notes in your own currency can be challenging at times, let alone introducing a set of notes that you've never seen before! Whilst the notes below aren't extensive, they can help you in determining whether notes are fake or not:

- Larger notes are more likely to be counterfeited; it's a better return on investment for counterfeiters.
- Examine the note, ideally against others of the same denomination, looking for imperfections such as texture in your hands, difference in colour, impurities in the printing process, missing / running ink (inspect your hands after handling the notes).
- Hold it up to the light to see if you can spot water marks or other security features Again, compare to similar notes if you can.

If in doubt, politely decline the note explaining that it looks damaged.

## Leftover cash at the end of the trip

If you travel to different parts of the world, you can amass a collection of coins and notes from different places. Airports sometimes have charity donation boxes / bins where you can donate surplus coins. You could consider being generous with tips at the end of the trip too

Some leftover currency can also be a souvenir of your trip as well. For example, notes sometimes can have depictions of the places that you have visited.

# Carrying US dollars / Euros / UK pounds

If you are traveling to developing parts of the world, it is a good idea to carry some major currency for converting if need be. Stick to US dollars, Euros, and sometimes UK pounds a these currencies have the greatest chance of being accepted. The amount to carry varies, however having enough to cover expected costs for a couple of days is a good minimum. The advantage of carrying this cash is that it can be reused elsewhere if you don't need it for this trip.

Think of this as a mini insurance policy, just in case you aren't able to use other means to ay for goods / services.

# Credit (and debit) cards

Whole books and websites are devoted to the topic of the value of credit cards when traveling. Without delving into which card is better for a scenario, or the general precautions around fraud risk (which apply anywhere), here are some international travel specifics with cards:

## Foreign exchange charges

Most merchant card readers are able to detect that your credit (or debit) card isn't a local one. It should provide a choice to the shop staff to allow you to pay either in the local currency, or the home currency that your card comes from. If you elect to have the charge in your home currency, the local merchant (i.e. the provider of the credit card machine) is going to charge you a commission (which will be a rubbish exchange rate). In addition, your credit card provided is also likely to charge you a foreign transaction fee for the "privilege" of using your card overseas (this is not a conversion fee cost). In other words, you will be hit with two fees in the end, without knowing what the local card merchant's fees are going to be.

If you choose to pay the transaction in the local currency, your own credit card provider will charge the currency conversion fee / rate, and potentially the transaction fee as well. Even though you may also get hit with two fees here, you can look up the credit card fees in advance and it's likely to be the cheaper of the two options.

## Card acceptance

Visa and MasterCard are the two credit card merchants that are most widely accepted around the world. American Express tends to be accepted in high-end hotels and restaurants, and not too many other places, in most of the world. Your chances of getting other cards (e.g. Diners Club, Discover, etc) accepted outside of the United States are often quite low.

## Contactless standards differ

Note that the uptake and usability of contactless payment methods can vary from country to country. In addition, your credit card provider may flag transactions as fraudulent even if they are low value. This could lead to your card being suspended and the hassle of getting it unlocked (or replaced).

# Travel cards

Pre-paid travel cards are generally available from banks and travel companies, often taking the form of a debit card. These cards are great for several reasons, although note that you do need to consider them as being the equivalent to cash (i.e. no protection for loss / theft):

- **One-time conversion fee -** You pay the conversion rate when you put money onto the card at the beginning of your trip. There are no subsequent conversions that need to be made.

- **Capped spending -** You can treat a travel card as a budgeting mechanism, in that you have a fixed amount loaded onto the card. When the money on the card is spent, there is no more money.

- **Capped exposure -** A side product of the point above is that if you were to lose your travel card, you have capped how much money you have lost.

# Exchanging or withdrawing money

There are several approaches to getting cash when traveling, and the pitfalls to consider are typically the same around the world. Not mentioned here are the issues associated with card readers in ATMs etc, which can happen in your own town as well as the other side of the world.

## Using ATMs

Assuming that your card is able to work overseas (a call to your bank can confirm this), withdrawing cash from an ATM can be a very convenient way of retrieving cash. ATMs around the world generally offer English language menus and can often detect the language in advance based on your card. Similar to the point above about conversion rates, it generally makes sense to ask the local bank to charge your bank in the local currency (you should be prompted on-screen for this). The exchange rates that ATMs use are often much more expensive than even what your bank will provide.

In countries where the currency contains lots of zeros, some ATMs will suggest withdrawal amounts that are excessive for regular use. Instead of being prompted with amounts such as $50, 100, 200 (or their equivalent), the starting rate is the equivalent of $500 (or more)! This is deliberately designed to trick unwitting tourists that assume that the lowest value listed must be the equivalent of the $20 / £20 back home. Look closely for this and have a clear number in mind that you intend to withdraw.

If in doubt, take your card and find another ATM.

> **Tip:** The sequence that ATMs provide cash and return the card to the customer can vary from country to country. Collecting your cash and card is such an unconscious action to most of us that if the sequence is out of sync, there's a solid chance we'll skip a step! If you are used to getting your card and then cash, when the sequence is reversed is when you'll run into problems. Because we expect to end the transaction with cash in our hands, we don't necessarily realise whether we've collected our card or not.
>
> Check to make sure you walk away from the ATM with cash and card!

## Airport / main train station currency vendors

If you can avoid these vendors, it's generally a good idea as they typically will offer the worst rates in the city. Make sure you are comfortable with the exchange rate and expect to pay a premium for the "convenience". If you are forced to use them for reasons of necessity or convenience, keep your wits about you. Or opt to convert the minimum amount that you need until you can get to a better currency exchange vendor.

## (Not) shopping around for the best rate

It can be tempting to hold out for an exchange rate that is better than the ones that you've seen so far. The reality is that the exchanges do talk to each other (or can even see each other) and generally don't have much of a difference in price between them. Don't be that person who ends up spending hours hunting for a bargain just to save a couple of dollars. Your time is worth more than this, particularly given you've travelled to a destination to take photos!

# TRANSPORT AND ACCOMMODATION TIPS

All of this preparation is now coming together for the actual trip. The first step is getting to your destination, which can often be the most stressful part of the entire trip. Here are some ways to approach your travel, depending on the mode(s) of transport that you are using, and where you are staying:

# FLIGHTS

Flying can be a pleasant experience for most people, and the journey itself can allow you to detach from the world below you and relax. In order to get yourself best set up for a smooth flight, here are some tried and tested approaches.

## Arrive at the airport early

This might feel like unnecessarily conservative advice, however nearly all of us feel some form of stress when it comes to flying. It might not be the flying itself, rather the whole process of going through an airport and sitting in a metal tube for hours on end surrounded by strangers. Our caveman ancestors didn't have such struggles. In any case, most airports have free WiFi and seating for you to sit down and have a read of your camera's manual (page 22).

## Airport security

If you're carrying a lot of camera equipment in your hand baggage, the odds of being picked out for a bag search are greater than the average passenger. It's sadly a fact of life for a traveling photographer, so it's easier to anticipate it and then not be disappointed. The security process generally isn't intrusive, it just adds 10-15 minutes to the amount of time it will take to get to the departure gate.

## Turn off data roaming on your mobile phone

The moment you switch your phone on at your destination, it will start hammering the first mobile phone carrier that it comes in contact with for as much data as it possibly can. Depending on your mobile phone carrier, this could VERY quickly become a huge chunk of change. Check out the "On the road" section (page 68) for alternative options to be able to keep receiving mobile phone data at your destination.

## Check-in online

Don't forget to check-in online, and if possible, choose your preferred seat. If it is a long-haul flight, you may have to consider the cost of purchasing a specific seat part of the overall ticket cost when choosing the airline. Unless you want to end up in the middle seat!

**Tip:** If you are going to be landing at your destination during the day, consider researching which side of the plane to sit on so that you will have great views of your destination as you come in to land. Keep your camera handy!

# DRIVING

Bearing in mind the points that we discussed when weighing up the advantages of hiring a car (page 48), here are some points for when you've picked up your car and are ready to go:

## Theft of belongings

This applies to anywhere, even with your own car at home. However, hire cars tend to have a "look" about them (if not the bumper stickers) that tells the world that they are a hire car, and so you don't need to get any would-be thief any extra reason to linger by your car. Don't leave your bags or equipment visible inside the car, putting them in the boot of the car, out of sight. Make sure that you don't leave anything inside of the car at night, particularly if it is parked in a public place.

## Local speed rules

The local tolerance for speeding varies widely from place to place. Keeping up with other traffic of itself isn't necessarily a guarantee that you'll avoid a surprise. In many countries, speed cameras tend to be affixed to tunnel entrances and exits, as well as entry / exit points to highways.

## Use of headlights

Depending on where you are, there could be a requirement that cars have their headlights on all of the time, even during the daytime. Check to see if your car is set up with automatic headlights, as sometimes during dawn and dusk it can be hard to determine if the lights are on or not. Often the headlight switch is near the steering column, and the car's manual should be in the glove box.

# ACCOMMODATION

The points below apply to staying in a hotel, AirBnB or similar, or even with friends and family in some cases. The more you are prepared for your trip, the less likely that you'll get caught out if something doesn't quite go to plan.

## The location of your accommodation

As we noted above, make sure your hotel booking record is easily accessible. It is also a good idea to mark your hotel on a map ahead of time, even if it's a book mark on a Google Map or similar. This can also help orient you with the destination, and you can visually show a taxi driver where you are wanting to go. Also consider taking a photo of the address card of the hotel so that you can share this with taxi drivers etc.

## Leaving baggage with the hotel

If you arrive prior to check-in, and your room isn't already available (some hotels may let you check in early), you should be able to leave your bags at reception before you go out exploring on day 1. It is a good idea to keep your passport on you, and don't leave it in a bag at the hotel reception.

## Hotel safe

If your hotel has a safe, consider using it for peace of mind. Make sure that you test its mechanism first, including setting a new PIN, closing, and then opening it, before you put any valuables inside. Note that most hotels will possess some form of master key to be able to unlock a safe, so consider it as a safety mechanism to stop the average thief / housekeeping rather than fool-proof. If in doubt, either carry the valuables on you, or leave them at home.

## Keeping hold of your passport

Asking for your passport to take a photocopy of the photo page is standard practise at hotels around the world. However, the hotel needing to keep a hold of your passport is not. Make sure that you avoid having to surrender your passport to the hotel staff as there should be no reason for them to keep it after they have a photocopy of your details.

## Check window locks

Once you have arrived in your room, do a quick inspection to make sure that everything is in order. Sometimes you can find that the locks on windows either don't work, or windows are left unlocked. This may particularly be the case for bathroom windows. If you're not in he room, it's a good idea to ensure that all windows are closed and locked.

## Consistency in your room habits

f you travel frequently, having habits for how you spread your stuff in a hotel room can go
 long way to ensuring that you can pack up to leave quickly, and that you're unlikely to
eave anything behind. This might mean leaving your dirty clothes in a pile together next to
our bag, your electronics chargers all plugged in one place, and wallet / purse on the
edside table.

## Ready to go

Vhen packing your bags, where possible put items that you'll need straight away in easily
ccessible spots. In particular make sure that camera equipment is readily accessible to head
ut from hotel as soon as you've arrived.

## Shower caps

Often one of the items in the complimentary toiletries that a hotel provides, shower caps
an be a great impromptu camera lens cover in the rain.

# ON THE ROAD

Perhaps the crux of this guide, the time spent on the ground in the destination should be both productive and fun. The travel photography tips and tricks below provide you with ideas to be thinking about. Like all of the other advice here, don't try to implement too many new things at once!

# PLANNING EACH DAY

The more that you plan the detail of each day of your trip, the greater the chance that you'll come away with the photos that you want, and you will feel satisfied that you have used your time effectively.

## Review your photo shot list

Earlier we covered creating your photo shot list (page 18) and reviewing it several times a day helps ensure that you don't miss any key photos that you had in mind. It can also help when looking at whether you need to adjust your itinerary based on what is left on the list.

## Prioritise sunrise and sunset

Make sure you know where you need to be in position for sunrise and for sunset, the times of the day with the best light on subjects. You may want to build into your daily itinerary time to return to your hotel to collect different equipment. By doing this, you can avoid having to lug your tripod around with you all day if you don't need it.

## Memory cards

Make sure that you swap memory cards in your camera every couple of days, even if they are only partly used. This is covered in more detail later (page 101).

## Take notes

This might include places that you've visited, opening hours, interesting facts, etc. Ways to capture notes include marking items on a physical map (hotels usually give you one), or by creating a Google Map to mark where you've been or taking a photo of location information / signs for later use. You can also make changes to your shot list (page 18) during your trip.

# Keep ticket stubs

It can be quite easy to amass a collection of entry tickets to the places that you've visited in a day, and often they feel like useless paper that you'll throw away at the earliest opportunity. If you hang onto this information, you can use it to record where you were (some tickets even have time stamps) so that you can identify your photos later on.

# Pack your bag the night before

Waking up at 4 am to catch the sunrise is difficult. Unless you possess the discipline of a Navy SEAL, you will need to do whatever you can to avoid the temptation of going back to bed / sleep. A big way that can help you is to set yourself up for success with your early morning routine. Make sure that your camera bag is all packed and ready to go. In addition, lay out your clothes for the day so that you just need to have a quick shower, get dressed, and you're out the door.

# Don't forget the spare batteries

This happens more than people would like to admit and will be more frustrating the further away from your hotel that you find yourself during the day! One way to combat this is to place the battery chargers on top of your camera bag when charging, to physically prompt you to put the batteries into the bag.

# GETTING THE PHOTOS THAT YOU IMAGINED

An old Chinese proverb says that "luck tends to favour the prepared", and this applies to taking photos. The following tips improve your odds of coming away from your trip with the photos that you want.

## Take the shot

Even if the light isn't fantastic, make sure you take the photo. If you're not sure it's interesting, still take the photo. You may not be presented with another opportunity to take the photo at a later stage, and sometimes the more mundane details can help round out the portfolio of your trip.

## Take lots of different photos

Memory card constraints aside, you can take an almost limitless number of photos. Well, technically speaking, your camera's shutter mechanism will eventually wear out; however, we digress...

Photos taken at different focal lengths, subjects, weather conditions, angles, all help to build the story of the place that you've visited. If the photos from your trip are purely front-on horizontal shots of buildings, they will have a limited appeal, and less likely to tell a story. Travel photos often tell a story as well as invoke emotional responses.

## Always bring a camera

At the very least, make sure that you've got your smart phone with its camera. You never know where inspiration will strike. A photo that is not technically brilliant is better than no photo. You might find that your favourite photo from a trip comes from a chance encounter, or something that made you laugh at the time. Even if it is the photo that you'll never share with the rest of the world, photos can have a deep meaning for you long after you've returned home.

## Look at (and potentially purchase) post cards

Make it a habit to pause and check out post cards whenever you pass a tourist shop. The photos on the post cards may not always be fantastic, however they visually show you the main sights to see, and potentially give a clue to the vantage point(s) for getting the best angle.

## Middle of the day heat / sun glare

For most subjects, direct overhead sunlight is often not very flattering. Highlights and shadows can be harsh, and often the contrast of bright areas and shade can be more than your camera can reasonably reproduce.

In addition, the early afternoon is typically the warmest time of the day, and locals in hot places know better than to be walking around in the direct heat. Consider falling in line with local custom, and retreat from the heat. Something to note is that in many places, museums and shops can be closed for lunch / early afternoon too.

This might be a good time to have a late lunch, or head back to your hotel for a rest. Overhead light can be best for shooting narrow streets and alleyways which tend to be thrown into harsh shadows for most of the day.

## Getting the geotag data

If you're lucky enough to own a camera with a built-in GPS (or with GPS attachment), then this won't apply to you. For the rest of us, there are a few different techniques that can be used to collect the GPS coordinates of where photos were taken, referred to as "geotagging" the photo. They are discussed in a later section (page 94).

Having geotag information for your photo allows you to know where the photo was taken. This may not sound valuable, however wading through hundreds (or thousands) of images trying to find a specific location is not a pleasant experience.

# WIFI AND MOBILE DATA

These days it feels like the bottom of the pyramid of Maslow's hierarchy of needs now includes "Free WiFi" (and "full battery")! There can be a bit of a philosophical debate as to whether being in a new place can be a good chance to unplug and explore without the world following you. Irrespective of which side of the argument you fall on, having data on your phone can serve several practical advantages when it comes to navigation and planning your days.

Two approaches that can be taken for getting data in a foreign country, assuming that your mobile phone carrier doesn't have a generous roaming plan available for you to use. Note that within European Union countries, the concept of data roaming has somewhat disappeared as carriers have to honour your data allowance across all EU countries.

Assuming that this doesn't apply to you, your first option to getting data on your phone is to swap out your regular SIM in your phone with a local SIM card purchased at your destination. This allows you to largely continue using your phone as-is. However, it means that you won't be able to send / receive calls and SMS messages from your normal phone number. In other words, you'll be less contactable. Depending on your perspective, this might actually be a good thing!

An alternative solution is to use an older phone that you've got lying around at home, one with the ability to act as a wireless hotspot. You can put a local SIM card into your old phone and connect your regular phone via WiFi. You'll be able to carry the old phone around in your camera bag, and your regular phone in your pocket as per normal. It will also mean that you can leave your phone in mobile roaming mode (with mobile data disabled, this is key!) so that you can send and receive calls.

A variation on the approach above is to buy / hire a wireless hotspot (also called a 3G / 4G router) and can pick up a local SIM card. The complication here is that carriers are a little less inclined to sell prepaid SIM cards with decent data allowances for WiFi hotspots as they expect that all of the data is more likely to be consumed.

**Tip:** Most larger airports will have a string of mobile phone retailers or vending machines with local SIM cards once you have collected your bags. Where possible, it is a good idea to get your SIM card sorted out at the airport as the prices will be the same (although perhaps with less plan options), and it means one less issue to deal with at a later time. In addition, staff at airport counters are much more likely to be able to speak English compared with stores that you may find in a city. Make sure that you keep your passport handy, as many countries will require that the mobile phone retailer takes a scanned copy of your passport.

# FITTING IN

The fact that you're a camera-toting tourist is likely to stand out, no matter where you are. However, there are several things that you can do to reduce the amount of friction between you and those that you come in contact. In many places, the locals are used to tourists, and probably have as much patience for them as you do for tourists in your hometown! Here are a few things that you can do to make life a little easier for all:

## Smile

It might be a cliché however a smile is universally understood and is universally reciprocated. Don't forget, you are in some new place with a chance to explore something that many people back home may only dream of! Smile, and the whole world smiles back at you.

## Learn the local language niceties

Being able to say "Hello" and "Thank you" should be your first priority. If possible, learn some basic nouns such as "toilet" and "bill" (cheque). Making that small effort alone could go a long way from differentiating you from the rest of the crowd.

## Ask before taking photos

This universal sign of respect of property and privacy seems to be all but forgotten by most people these days. You don't have to be that person, and often if you ask or gesture at your camera, many people actually enjoy posing for you.

## Try the local food

For many travellers, this is going to be the highlight if not the entire reason for their trip. Food tells so much about a culture, and also some clues about the world that they inhabit. Like any other type of photo, lighting is going to be key to getting the best shots of your food and drinks. In restaurants, ask to sit near windows with strong light if possible. Consider even using the torch function on your smartphone to provide a bit of extra light onto a subject, which will look more visually appealing than on-camera flash.

## Try the local drinks

Similar to the point above about food, drinking is often a social ritual. This can range anywhere from a pint at the pub in the United Kingdom to a Japanese tea ceremony. The added challenge with shooting drinks can come from reflections on the drink glass, for which on-camera flash is going to produce the most glare. If you are resorting to using an on-camera flash, try to place a sheet of tissue paper or thin white paper in front of the flash. This will act as a cheap diffuser which can produce a much more flattering light, albeit not as powerful a light.

# GENERAL TRAVEL PHOTOGRAPHY TIPS

The following tips are designed to help make your trip as smooth and enjoyable as possible, and many are ultimately common sense.

## Pacing

As much as you might be treating the trip as a photo assignment, know your physical (and emotional) limits. If you don't do much exercise in your regular life, expecting to be pounding the streets all day without feeling sore later will only set you up for pain later on. Be realistic about what you can cover in a day and plan your trip accordingly. As discussed previously (page 14), you are usually able to return at another time if there's more to taken in than one trip alone.

## Be flexible

Similar to the point above, your plans need to have a degree of flexibility, particularly if you're wanting to capture places in the best light. Unless you're visiting somewhere that has guaranteed sunshine and brilliant weather every day, sometimes the weather is just not going to be on your side. There are many ways to work within this constraint (page 68), however it might mean that you'll need to re-order the priority of what you are going to see.

## Tourist information centres

Your hotel is likely to have plenty of brochures and pamphlets tempting you with all sorts of local activities and sights. The challenge can sometimes come in actually booking tours or access to specific locations. Tourist information centres should be in a good position to help you and are most likely going to have English-speaking staff.

## Dress appropriately

When you know that you're going to be visiting places of worship, err on the side of conservatism (and respect) and ensure that you're wearing clothing that covers your upper arms and also down to your knees. Some places can have greater requirements than this, particularly for women. As a rule, the more conservative the location, the more clothing that needs to be worn.

## Avoiding tour groups

Here is the tour group modus operandi: tours take their groups about in coaches, park in big car parks, and let them loose on an attraction for a prescribed 45 minutes plus 15 minutes of toilet break! In order to keep costs down, most tour groups tend to stay in hotels that are a little further out, and so they will only have rounded up the guests and bussed them into the city sometime after breakfast.

If you want a place to yourself, your best bet is to get there when the street sweepers are doing their morning shift, usually around sunrise. You will be surprised the number of popular places (including many major cities / capitals) that are almost empty if you are up a little earlier than most, from New York City's Grand Central Station to Venice's Piazza San Marco.

## Left baggage lockers

An alternative to leaving your bags at the hotel reception when you arrive or on your day of departure is to use the left baggage facilities found at most major train stations and bus terminals. This is a particularly good idea if your route home (or back to the airport) takes you in this direction anyway, and it means that you avoid having to double back to your hotel to collect bags.

## Visible lock on your camera bag

Personal safety is important no matter where you go, and there are many precautions that you should take to ensure that you are not putting yourself in unnecessary danger at any time. Whether you decide to lock your camera bag when walking around is up to you and how comfortable you feel. Do note that the downsides of this are that a visible lock can make your bag of more interest to a would-be pickpocket. More likely is that the constant unlocking and locking the bag will start to frustrate you quite quickly.

What is perhaps a more flexible approach is to place your valuables (e.g. passport) in an internal pocket that is only accessed from an inside zip. This is going to be very difficult for somebody to access without you being aware.

# Google Maps lists

Marking out the places that you wish to visit makes the map reading process much more efficient. It also allows you quickly mark down places that you've identified during the day that you wish to return to when the light is better / different. The Google Maps "List" comes to the rescue (it will even work for offline maps).

Note: You will need a Google account, and be signed-in to use this functionality. The good news is that the list is automatically available across all devices that you are logged in to.

**Bonus:** We have created a step-by-step tutorial for creating a new Google Maps list and adding items to this list. The tutorial includes screenshots to help explain the details.

To get your free step-by-step tutorial, head over to
walkaboutphotoguides.com/travelphotosplanning/bonuses

# END OF EACH DAY

After your day of shooting is done, you may be very glad to see the inside of your hotel room and a comfortable bed. Before you give in to temptation to get a good night of sleep, don't forget to do the following:

## Charging batteries

Setting out early morning to discover your camera battery has no juice will not set a good tone for your day! Even if you've not used your camera much during the day, the habit of charging everything at night is one that is best adopted. Make sure you recharge your phone and any other electronic devices that you rely on, every night.

## Downloading photos

If you have brought a laptop or tablet with you, don't forget to make your first backup of the photos taken during the day. Check out the section on managing your photos when traveling (page 101) for more information.

## Review your photos

Similar to practising your technique before you go on a trip (page 21), taking the time to review your photos can serve as an invaluable learning tool. Critically look at each photo, taking in elements such as composition and story. Did you get the photo that was in your mind / vision (barring adjustments in post-processing)? If not, what was missing? This can range from technical considerations such as shutter speed not fast enough (page 26) to wrong choice of lens for the scene (page 96).

Viewing the EXIF data (page 109) of a photo can give you some clues as to what went wrong if the issue is a technical one. Or, the reason that you aren't quite satisfied with a photo can come down to good old-fashioned patience, waiting for people / objects to align in a pleasing manner.

As you review your photos, make sure that you take notes on what you observe, and pick out 1-2 changes that you will make for the following day. Any more than 1 or 2 changes will likely result in you tying yourself in knots trying to fix everything and end up changing nothing.

## Identify what photos you missed / still need

Take note of places that you didn't quite get the photos that you wanted and note for potential changes in your itinerary. Similar to the point above about patience, you may need to adjust the time of day that you get to a location to take a shot. Or wait for the weather gods to smile on you, it can be as basic as that.

## Swap memory cards in camera

This is a great habit to get into, particularly because memory cards are cheap these days. Don't use the same card for more than a day or two, and swap them out when they are 75% full at the end of a day. And whatever you do, don't delete anything from your memory cards until you've got home. If you get desperate for space, consider paying a little more and purchasing additional cards from tourist shops rather than deleting photos.

## Check your alarm clock

Before you get some well-deserved sleep, make sure that you've set your alarm clock(s) for the morning. Give yourself a little extra margin of time than anticipated for getting ready and getting to your destination. If you're chasing a sunrise, your window of opportunity can be merely minutes so being early does tend to pay off.

# END OF YOUR TRIP

Returning back to reality from a holiday is always tough, and photography trips are generally no different. The good news is that not only do you have the memories of your trip, you'll have a set of photos that you will be able to start sharing with the world. There are a few tips to help you along the way, and then you can get stuck into post-processing.

# AS SOON AS POSSIBLE

There are some tasks, mostly administrative in nature, that make a lot of sense to complete at the earliest opportunity once you are back at your home base. Many of the tasks may feel obvious, however we have captured them here for completeness:

## Copy memory cards

This is where your photo management workflow will really help you out. Depending on your setup, and your level of paranoia (!), making sure that you have at least two permanent copies of all photos is being cautious and sensible. This is covered in more detail later (page 104).

## Wash your clothes

This might feel like your parent speaking! However, chances are that your clothes have come back a little sweaty from the walking around and exercise during the trip. Considering that you may have been to another part of the world (or at least, somewhere far away), washing your clothes reduces the chances of you introducing a foreign nasty into your home environment. Plus, it will smell better!

Don't forget items such as hats, scarves, gloves, face washers, towels, and other items that may have come in contact with your body along the way. And if you're feeling particularly energetic, giving your shoes and boots a clean is always a good idea.

## Notes from your trip

There are several aspects of your trip that you may want to remember for later, and as time goes on, your ability to recall the specifics of your trip will diminish. Capturing notes is particularly helpful if you are looking to create social media content based on your trip and want to remember either the sequence of events of particular stories. Write down notes of where you visited, particularly if you don't have geotag data of your photos.

# Unpack

Similar to the point above about washing your clothes, unpacking your photography gear allows it to "breathe" normally, and reduce the chances of condensation building up in lenses. Nothing ruins electronics (or film for that matter) like the effects of water, so you'll be improving the lifespan of your beloved equipment.

# WHAT TO DO WITH ALL OF YOUR PHOTOS

Now that you've spent all of this time, energy, and money, it is time to start bringing your work to life and sharing with the world. As a general rule, the sooner you get your photos into some sort of order, the easier it will be over time to manage the photos and use them.

# PROCESSING WORKFLOW

The terms "processing workflow" or "post-processing" are somewhat interchangeable when it comes to photography. Your cameras are excellent at capturing images. However, they are typically pretty useless at categorising the images into anything other than date taken. Once you've started accumulating a photo collection over time, sorting purely by date can tax the best of minds in remembering the dates of each of your trips!

# WORKFLOW MANAGEMENT TOOLS

A photography workflow management tool allows you to move beyond simple file management into logical categorisation tools for your images, and groups of images. You can use a workflow management tool to create tags (labels) for your photos, allowing you to find themes / people at a later date, which can often save a lot of time. Workflow management is considered different to photo editing, although many of the key tools (discussed below) do overlap a fair bit between the two.

## Integrated image management and photo editors

Like everything in life, you get what you pay for, and the industry standard tools do come with a price tag. Here are the most common tools for combined image management as well as some photo editing:

### Adobe Lightroom Classic CC

Lightroom Classic CC comes as part of an Adobe Creative Cloud subscription. This is considered the industry standard photography workflow tool, and the most widely used by photographers. Catalogue management and JPEG / Raw photo enhancement are its bread-and-butter, however there's also a variety of publishing features (Web, Print, Book, Slideshow).

Available as part of the Adobe Creative Cloud Photography subscription.

Cloud-based: No
Windows: Yes
Mac: Yes
Linux: No
Android: Yes
iOS: Yes

## Adobe Lightroom CC

Lightroom CC comes as part of an Adobe Creative Cloud subscription. It is a cloud-based (online), stripped-down version of Lightroom Classic CC. Your photos are stored in the Adobe cloud, with 1Tb of storage included in the subscription price (varies by country). This solution is best suited to those who prefer to edit their photos on their mobile devices, and don't want to spend time sitting at a computer during the editing process.

Cloud-based: Yes
Windows: No
Mac: No
Linux: No
Android: No
iOS: No

## Adobe Bridge

Taking many of the photo library management elements of Adobe Lightroom CC / Classic CC and serving up in a free package, what's not to like? Photo editing is very basic however this can be supplemented with other tools described here.

Cloud-based: No
Windows: Yes
Mac: Yes
Linux: No
Android: No
iOS: No

## Skylum Luminar

A recent addition to the market, Skylum (formerly Macphun) Luminar now comes with image library management as of end of 2018.
Cloud-based: No
Windows: Yes
Mac: Yes
Linux: No
Android: No
iOS: No

## Cyberlink Photodirector

A low-cost alternative to Adobe's subscription offering, Photodirector has a variety of cataloguing capabilities as well as photo editing. Make sure that the application supports your camera(s) and / or lenses as it's not as comprehensive as other options listed here.

Cloud-based: No
Windows: Yes
Mac: Yes
Linux: No
Android: No
iOS: No

## Capture One Pro

Traditionally seen as a pro photographer's go-to for tethered shooting (where the camera is connected to a laptop / tablet for real time results / review), Capture One Pro has now branched out. It has library management as well as comprehensive photo editing capabilities. Many professional photographers are migrating to Capture One Pro due to its advanced functionality.

Cloud-based: No
Windows: Yes
Mac: Yes
Linux: No
Android: No
iOS: No

# Photo editors

There is a myriad of software options available for editing your photos, particularly if you are shooting in JPEG format (and not Raw). Similar to the list above, the more comprehensive options typically will have a higher cost either up-front or through a subscription model.

Some of the more popular stand-alone photo editors include:

- **Adobe PhotoShop -** Powerful desktop-focused image editor, available as part of the Adobe Creative Cloud Photography subscription.

- **RawTherapee -** Free PhotoShop alternative that's open source and runs on Linux (as well as Windows / Mac).

- **Snapseed -** Easy to use mobile / tablet editor for editing on the go, or those who prefer the more tactile approach.

Don't forget that you can also use the in-built photo editor that comes with your operating system for basic edits.

# ORGANISING YOUR FILES

Once you've established which workflow management tool you want to use, you will need to think about how to logically order your images. The ways that you can achieve this are described below, without being too tool-specific, for each catalogue. The typical language that is used to describe categorisation is Catalogue / workspace -> Collection set / group -> Collection /category

The idea is that you group photos together that are in some way thematically linked, allowing you to find similar photos relatively easily. For example, having one catalogue (top-level point of separation) for each European country may not make sense if you only went on one European trip!

## By location

For travel photography, this is going to be the most logical way to group your photos together. How often you travel to a location may affect how you want to differentiate between locations. For example, if you only take that one European bus tour, you may want to divide your photos up by country, or perhaps major city.

The big benefit of ordering by location means that all of your photos of Shanghai taken over the years are all in the same place. This is particularly helpful if the subjects that you most like to photograph don't tend to change much over time (e.g. historic buildings and monuments, animals, etc.).

## By event

Using the example above, the event could be "European holiday 2018" as your catalogue, and collections by major city. If you also shoot event photography (weddings, corporate functions, etc), then arranging by event will make a lot of sense to you.

## By date

For those of us with phenomenal memories, organising your photos by date may make sense. Sorting by date tends to be most useful for technical reference information, however it doesn't quite lend itself to travel photography. In such cases you may be able to get away with your operating system's file manager (such as Windows Explorer) acting as your workflow management tool.

## Hybrid approach

An example of a hybrid approach could be to combine location and event information into your categorisation system. You could start with a high-level catalogue of "Africa" and then create collection sets by trips that you have made, assuming that you don't make too many trips.

The technicalities on how to create and manage your files will vary to a degree between workflow management tools, and so is outside of the scope of this guide.

# EDITING YOUR PHOTOS

Editing your photos is an entire industry of itself! The tips below are some high-level points to consider, and there are some amazing resources out there to explain in-depth how to use each photo-editing tool to get the most out of your photos.

The concept of Raw vs. JPEG image files is discussed in more detail below (page 93), however you will be able to eek a lot more information out of your Raw images during the edit process than JPEG files.

When it comes to using a phone vs. tablet vs. PC/Mac for editing, this can essentially be considered, to a degree, a speed vs quality decision. For images shot on a phone or tablet, your best bet is to edit the photo on the same device that you used to take it. This is going to be straightforward for you and allow you to have a "finished" product ready for sharing in the shortest time possible.

Where PC or Mac photo editing come into their own is when you want to focus more on the quality of the output, particularly for larger files. This doesn't mean that phone and tablet photos are rubbish, it is just that they do not compete with DSLRs and mirrorless cameras when it comes to image quality. A PC or Mac is typically a much more powerful device, giving you much greater latitude with how you edit your photos and the level of complexity that can be applied. In addition, it is much easier to connect a PC or Mac up to a large screen, allowing you to better inspect the detail in a photo.

# SAVING YOUR PHOTOS

Now that your hard work has produced images that you are ready to share with the world, don't forget to save them somewhere first! Depending on the original file format of your photo (Raw vs JPEG), the editing process may have already overwritten the original photo. You can often elect to save an edited image separately, and where possible, this should be your preferred approach. This gives you the ability to return at a later date to edit again. You may choose to re-edit your photos because your editing skills have further improved, or perhaps you're in a position to use a more powerful editor for the image.

In any case, apply the same level of rigour to backing up the edited images as you have done for the originals that you captured in the first place. This will save you countless hours and heartache if there is a corruption of your files that occurs at some stage.

# PUBLISHING ON SOCIAL MEDIA

The ways and means to reach your audience via social media are huge. Rather than go into the nitty gritty of how to post to Instagram, Facebook, YouTube, Twitter, your blog, e-Newsletter, snail mail, your grandmother's garden club newsletter, etc., let's talk about some types of photos that you may want to think twice about sharing. Some of these types of images could cause unexpected complications because of legal reasons or copyright restriction. Some complications could come about because of cultural sensitivity, which can differ widely from place to place. You may read these concepts below and assume that they are common-sense, and yet, there is sadly plenty of examples online to demonstrate otherwise.

The following may come across as quite morbid and / or patronising, however it is trying to cover many bases for readers from different parts of the world. If you get to the end of this section without having picked up any tips, then chances are you are already a well-versed global citizen, so go and celebrate!

# COPYRIGHT OR LEGAL CONSIDERATIONS

Depending on the way that you're sharing your photos, copyright or legal considerations can quickly become a minefield! Assuming that we aren't talking about selling your photos (page 89), many places and countries have restrictions on how your photos can be used.

## Copyright restrictions

Here are a couple of starter links to find out whether the photo that you've taken is subject to copyright restrictions:

### Adobe Stock Contributors website

Copyright for a collection of known (i.e. popular) locations and subjects:
https://helpx.adobe.com/stock/contributor/help/known-image-restrictions.html

### Shutterstock Contributors website

Copyright for a collection of known (i.e. popular) locations and subjects:
https://www.shutterstock.com/contributorsupport/articles/kbat02/Known-Image-Restrictions

Something to note is that different countries consider the use of images and video on YouTube / Instagram, or other publicly facing services as potentially commercial use. Some locations expect that you seek permission to use photos and video for anything other than "personal consumption" (which can be a bit of a vague term!). The good news is that the vast majority of places that do have restrictions the use of images and video taken on their premises do have information on their website explaining the rules and how to proceed.

To protect yourself, as a general rule, ensure that the image / video used isn't directly being associated with a product / service that you are trying to sell. In addition, that the photograph doesn't give an impression that the people in the photo are endorsing something that you are sharing.

The following types of photographs, whilst potentially legally taken, may still cause some controversy if improperly shared publicly. Two key pointers here:

- If in doubt, don't share it!
- Ensure that any potentially controversial image is appropriately curated to make it clear that it isn't exploiting the subject in any way.

In most instances where there has been some violation, you'll be asked to take down the offending image(s). Quick and friendly compliance is much less likely to result in legal action (which is typically seen as a last resort option).


# POVERTY

For large numbers of people around the world, poverty is sadly a core part of their existence. Visiting certain places will invariably expose you to conditions that you may find disturbing and / or heart-wrenching. It would be naïve and perhaps do injustice to a location to simply ignore the realities of how people are living.

However, there is a difference between taking photos to represent somewhere that you've travelled to, and what can be termed "poverty porn". This refers to instances where images that are taken in such a way that would suggest that the photographer hasn't bothered to engage with the subject, rather they have essentially shot the subject in the photo in the same way as a zoo animal - simply taking their photo and moving on.

This can also include cliché photos that are often linked to "voluntourists" (tourists performing some modicum of volunteer effort). These clichés can include the tourist posing with a group of smiling children somewhere in Africa, etc. It may have been a genuine moment, however the court of public opinion (aka social media) can quite quickly get the wrong idea and the facts surround the image quickly take a back seat.

**Tip:** As to whether you take the image or not, this might want to be something that you have a general rule for (e.g. no photos of begging). What can be helpful is to have some hard-and-fast rules around when to not take photos when you're out and about. This can help avoid issues at the time, as well as later on when considering which photos to publish.

# DEATH / THE DEAD

One of the characteristics that separates humans from almost all other mammals is our rituals involving the recognition of death. This is an intense time for anyone affected by the passing of a person (or even an animal) and can be particularly traumatic if it is the death of a young person or somebody who has died unexpectedly.

The funeral rituals or ceremonies that are performed to honour and remember the dead are a key part of all major religions, and to an outsider may be considered fascinating from a cultural perspective. However, it is still people at their potentially most vulnerable, and should be afforded the same courtesy and respect as you would expect to receive if it was your friend or relative that had passed away. This ties in with the section above about poverty.

Expanding this idea, in some places taking photographs in a cemetery is considered inappropriate, even if no people are visible in the photo. The legality and acceptability of this can vary widely. There are cities that hold tours of cemeteries in their city, and then other cemeteries in the same city don't allow photography at all! If there are restrictions on photography, or the use of these images, the cemetery typically provides warnings at the entrance gate, or on their website.

# RELIGIOUS CEREMONIES / RITUALS

As a general rule, you should not photograph people who are in prayer, even if they are not inside a place of worship. This is a very personal time for an individual, when they are in communication with their deity(s). The invasion of their privacy won't be welcome.

Completely going the other direction, festive religious ceremonies such as weddings, Baptisms, Christenings, Bar Mitzvahs, etc., don't have issues with photography. If anything, photos are encouraged! Just try not to interfere with any of the ritualistic elements, for example if the camera shutter of your camera is louder than anyone speaking!

# ILLEGAL ACTIVITY / PROTEST

This is a tough point of wrap your mind around, as it may not always be clear what is an illegal act in some countries. Consider this scenario – you capture pictures of somebody (or a group) protesting, and then share these pictures on social media. These pictures could subsequently be used by the state security services of that country to identity the individuals involved. Although completely unintended, you could be contributing to some fairly serious negative consequences for the individuals who were in your photos.

# ANIMAL CRUELTY

This doesn't specifically refer to torturing animals, which are clearly offensive and / or distressing to any viewer! What is being discussed here are types of animal photography that can feel more prosaic, or perhaps not even a concern from your standpoint. Whilst there may be some philosophical or moral concerns at play, the list below are types of photos that include animals that could sometimes not be universally enjoyed:

## Circus / performing animals

Many readers will have had fond memories of going to see animals perform at the circus as part of childhood. In a lot of cases, the animals do get treated humanely, and are regularly looked after by both keepers and vets. However, there are instances where the activities that animals are made to perform run very contradictory to their nature, and so torture or beating (or the threat thereof) are the method that is used to constrain an otherwise wild animal. As an example, jumping through a ring of fire is not a natural act (think of a lion leaping through a burning ring), nor is fighting with barbs strapped to the feet (cock fighting).

## Animals being ridden

Increasingly, there is an awareness that tourists riding animals such as elephants can subject these gentle creatures to cruel treatment and pain at the hands of their keepers. A lot of tourists are opting instead to have other encounters with animals such as feeding, washing, or simply patting them, rather than riding.

## Meat of certain animals

We humans seem to have a fondness for many animals (e.g. pandas, monkeys, pets), and so can find a photographic reminder of others eating such animals to be quite distressing or off-putting. Examples of this include eating the flesh / meat of turtle, tortoise, dolphin, whale, cat, dog, as well as endangered animals.

## Animals hunting in the wild

This refers to witnessing nature at play, such as predators capturing prey on safari. If you choose to post such images or video, make sure that you place a warning so that viewers can elect whether to view the content or not. This could be done through classifying it as "adult" material so that (in theory) children won't be able to access it.

# NUDITY

Taking photos of nude individuals, and sharing them publicly, risks violating that individual's privacy, not to mention likely legal (and safety) consequences. There are places where people generally have an expectation that they are afforded a degree of privacy such in their home (including backyard), nude beaches, shower rooms / changing areas, spas, etc. In fact, there are very few places where you can expect to see people naked that would be considered appropriate for you to take a photo!

In addition, if the person is under 18 years old (or looks it), you are inviting some very serious consequences if you are in possession of such photos, let alone if you post them!

# CHILDREN

Photographing children can sometimes be problematic, not just because they don't stand still long enough to get a shot! It is best to seek permission from parents / guardians beforehand. This could be as simple as making eye contact with the parents and gesturing towards your camera. Alternatively, group shots of kids are much less of a hassle or intimidating, and make sure that you crouch down to their eye level to get the best angle. Show the children the image you just took on the LCD screen of the camera, and their smiles will light up your day!

# WOMEN

In some conservative societies, it is not acceptable for men to make eye contact with women, let alone photograph them. It will usually be quite apparent to you that there are restrictions on the types of photos that you can take, so if in doubt, ask first. Getting caught taking photos of women in such circumstances can very quickly escalate into a dangerous situation, so it is best avoided.

# SELLING TRAVEL PHOTOGRAPHS

With the ubiquity of camera phones these days, your ability to sell a photo is made that much harder than in the days of film when not too many people took photos.

# PHOTOS THAT ARE LIKELY TO BE IN DEMAND

The following are generally the types of travel photos that are likely to sell:

## National / international events

This tends to morph into the realm of photojournalism, which is a bit different to travel photography. However, if you happen to be at the right place at the right time to capture the moment, news agencies might be willing to pay money for it. You'll need to approach them with the photo and be able to demonstrate that you are the original author of the photo (i.e. you own the copyright). It is also going to be key that you demonstrate that the photo has not been altered in any way, usually the JPEG image (page 93).

## Unique locations / scenes

Your photo of New York City's Times Square is unlikely to stand out; that's just reality these days. However, if you're able to convey far less frequented places in a pleasing manner, then this can be of interest to buyers. In particular, capturing photos of "up and coming" travel destinations can be a good idea to make a little cash.

## Natural phenomena

If you've got a brilliant take on Arora Borealis (the Northern lights) or a great perspective shot of a red moon, you might be able to find an audience.

In short, it's unlikely that travel photos are your ticket to becoming a millionaire. Usually it is the accompanying stories that are what help sell images to audiences or help build a following on social media platforms.

# STOCK PHOTOGRAPHY

A myriad of stock services (Getty Images, Shutterstock, Adobe Stock, Alamy) exist that act as the market makers between photographers and buyers. A warning: they do take a sizeable cut of the action, so even if you manage to get 50% of the sale price you are doing pretty well! Similar to the points above, here are some ways to improve the chances of your photos being accepted for collections, and subsequently sold:

## Commercial use

The difference between editorial use and commercial use of photos can become complex to navigate. In simplistic terms, almost any photograph can be editorial in nature as it is simply reflecting reality at a point in time. In addition, editorial can also include composite images (lots of post-processing) or images that are in fact artworks rather than photos, so long as you acknowledge that the image has been altered.

The (non-legal) way to describe the commercial use of a photo is that the photograph can be used to sell a product / service. In order to do this, there cannot be copyrighted objects that are the main focus of a photo (without permission from the manufacturer / owner), and that there are model releases in place for any people and / or recognisable buildings that are prominently featured. A commercial use photo can be used to sell a product and / or service, and therefore any objects in the photo can be assumed to be associated with the product / service being sold. This is why model / property releases are key.

## High quality

Your images much be of a high quality; this is a given. Stock agencies are incredibly strict about the quality of the images that they will accept. Photos taken on camera phones can sometimes struggle to be sold as they aren't so good quality when viewed on a larger monitor. The same applies to photos that are "noisy" (page 112), with higher-end cameras are typically much better at reducing the effects of camera noise.

## Unique

If you are the only person with a killer photo that is relevant to a buyer's need, then chances are they'll go for your photo. The more appealing, unique, and relevant to the buyer's need, the better. Stock agencies typically will let existing contributors know what sort of images are in demand, often aligning with seasons of the year.

> **Tip:** If you're looking for which stock agencies that you'd like your images to be sold on, keep an eye out for existing photos that you see in media and look at their attribution. The news agency will always attribute the photograph to the agency that sold the image, and sometimes even the author of the photo.

**Advanced tip:** The main reason that that most editorial stock photos get rejected by agencies is because the images are not "clean" enough. To avoid this, make sure you use the lowest ISO possible for the photo, and keep any post-processing to the minimum. The "processed" look is largely to be avoided as it doesn't sell in the real world. In addition, tastes in images change over time, and having an image that is more realistic looking tends to "age" better than an image that has been processed based on the tastes of the day.

# SELL FROM YOUR SOCIAL MEDIA PLATFORMS

If you already have a sizeable following on social media platforms including your blog or Instagram, your audience may be interested in purchasing your photos. You can sell them a full-size digital copy of a photo, or perhaps you want to provide a printed and / or framed copy and mail them out.

# CAMERA REFERENCE GUIDE

This camera reference guide is designed to give an overview of the different types of cameras out there, typical settings, and other tips and techniques. It is always good practice to familiarise yourself with the manual for your camera and any key accessories (e.g. flashes) to best understand their capabilities.

# BASIC CAMERA SETTINGS

A quote often used in the photography world is that "the best camera is the one that's with you". If you are reading this guide, and indeed this section, you are looking to get the best performance out of the camera(s) that you have, which is a great attitude to have. After all, a Ferrari does not make you a better driver by default!

Your camera can broadly fit into one of the following categories (for simplicity):

- Smartphone camera
- "Point and shoot" (P&S) camera
- "Bridge" camera
- Mirrorless camera
- DSLR camera

Out of the box, these cameras (with the exception of smart phones without zoom capability) are all capable of taking a multitude of different photos. This means having the right lens attached, appropriate accessories, and good lighting. Things do get a little trickier with smartphones and a P&S, however they have the distinct advantage of being the camera most likely with you for any occasion.

A simple breakdown of the different modes for your camera, which smartphones can simulate (using camera apps):

- **Auto -** Used in times when you want the photo without any of the hassle. This works well for simple, evenly-lit scenes. It also works well when there is so much going on that getting an imperfect shot is generally better than getting no shot!

- **Aperture priority -** Used when you want to control the depth of field of a shot, from portraits (blurring out the background) to landscapes (capture the most detail in the frame).

- **Shutter priority -** Ideal for instances when you want to freeze the action or see the world faster than the blink of an eye. Or capture children or animals; they move QUICKLY.

- **Manual priority -** When you want to show your camera who is boss! Great for long exposures, amongst other more advanced tasks.

Shooting in Manual-mode doesn't mean that you're necessarily any better at taking photos, so don't feel that you're not able to achieve anything if you're using Auto mode. The key is that you get the shot that is in your mind using the most appropriate mode and camera functions. At the end of the day, the camera is a tool to help realise your vision.

# RAW VS. JPEG – WHICH FORMAT SHOULD I USE?

Nothing seems to divide the photography community more than whether to shoot Raw or JPEG; this is similar to the "which camera is best?" question. If you want to set off an intense debate, ask two (or more) photographers which is better. Once you've lopped this conversational grenade into their midst, be prepared for tears, name calling, and occasionally, even facts!

The term "Raw" can be thought of as a digital version of a film negative from traditional cameras. Similar to a film negative, the Raw file is not viewable in its native format and will need to be "developed" to get the desired image. Raw images retain all of the visual information that the camera sensor captured when the shutter button was pressed, and therefore more can be achieved with the final image during development (also known as post-processing).

A JPEG image is a Raw image that has been automatically developed by the software in the camera to produce an image that appears sharper, has greater contrast, and colours that "pop". This means that the JPEG image will appear much more pleasing straight out of the camera.

Raw files will give you the greatest options for post-processing images and getting the most out of the information that the camera sensor captured. Most cameras these days do a very good job of automatically capturing great photos in JPEG format in-camera. In addition, JPEG photos will take up significantly less space on your memory cards.

For certain applications, such as news reporting, agencies only accept the JPEG photos taken straight out of the camera. This is because the JPEG photos are available straight away in a "final" version ready for publication, where speed is of the essence. In addition, there is much less opportunity for image tampering associated with JPEG images (modification of the image is much harder and more obvious) thus retaining the integrity of the image. This is a core tenet of photojournalism.

Consider your use case for your images. If in doubt about what you'll use the images for at some future point, shoot in Raw. Just remember to carry more memory cards as Raw images take up more space.

# GEOTAGGING YOUR IMAGES

Wouldn't it be fantastic if you knew where each of your photos was taken so that you didn't need to wrack your brains to remember which museum / temple / country a photo was taken in! One of the distinct advantages of using the camera in your phone is that most smartphones automatically embed GPS information into the photo's information (called the "EXIF data"). Adding the GPS data is referred to as geotagging and is incredibly helpful for sorting through large numbers of photos when looking for an image of a location. Geotagging your photos is possible in three main ways, listed below.

## In-camera

We talked about smartphones above, and there are a select number of bridge and DSLR cameras that come with a built-in GPS. You may need to spend a little time waiting for the camera to get sufficient GPS signal in order for geotagging to start working. Usually, the further away from the last place that you used the camera, the longer the process is going to take to get a GPS signal. In addition, getting a GPS signal indoors is all but impossible.

Sadly, a built-in GPS is not a common feature found on modern DSLRs and mirrorless cameras, for a few different reasons. The GPS unit adds to the cost, and potentially the weight of the camera, and it is one more component that will drain the camera's battery, when battery life can often be a key selling point. And lastly, the demand for GPS in most cameras doesn't seem to be there in the market.

For many Canon and Nikon DSLRs, a rather expensive add-on unit can be purchased which fits to the hot shoe of the camera and automatically records geotag information for the photos taken by the camera. Fortunately for Sony mirrorless camera owners, there is a solution available that connects your camera via BlueTooth to your smartphone to get GPS data.

## Geo-tracking device

Using some form of geo-tracking software on your phone or a dedicated GPS unit allows you to match up the GPS data for a day with the timestamp of photos that were taken with your camera. This requires that you sync your camera's internal time / date mechanism with the GPS recording device, which will get its time from GPS satellites and so their time will be highly accurate. You will need to carry the geo-tracking device with you as you take photos.

Once you've returned to your photography workflow software, you upload both your photos as well as the geo-tracking data. Your workflow tool can then take the geo-tracking data and embed the associated GPS data against photos based on the timestamp of each photo (your camera will record this). More advanced workflow software can correct for time sync issues including time zones as well as a camera with a slow / fast clock.

# Manual geotagging

No sugar-coating – this process can be laborious and painful. This requires you to remember where a particular photo was taken and then use geotagging software to drag-and-drop the photos onto maps to then embed the geotag information into the photo. This manual process can work well for a small number of locations or photos. However, it will quickly become painful if you've spent a day exploring a city!

# CAMERA LENSES AND ACCESSORIES

Here is a breakdown of the types of lenses and accessories that you'll typically use for travel photography.

# LENSES

Your choice of lens for a particular shot includes several considerations, mainly:

- **Closeness to the subject -** Think of this as the amount of "zoom" in an image. Apart from being able to see objects that are far away with more detail (or very close up), a zoom allows you to take a photo without interfering with the scene. Or not having to get too close to that lion!

- **The distance between the subject and the background -** This may not be so obvious a consideration for many people. Very wide and very long (zoom) lenses can help either exaggerate or compress proportions of objects. See below about specific lenses and their effect on an image.

- **Available light -** All other things being equal, it is harder to take a well composed (and sharp) photo at 300mm than at 30mm. This means that it is easier to take photos in low-light conditions with a wide-angle lens than a tele-zoom.

The information below describes the typical use cases for different types of lenses used for travel photography. There are additional lens types not mentioned here as they aren't commonly used, and so don't often make sense to travel with, such as:

- **Fisheye lens -** Incredibly wide field of view, although the image will have a distorted "fisheye" look. This can often be corrected (to an extent) using post-processing.

- **Macro lens -** Similar to a prime lens (page 98), a macro lens is fantastic for close-up images as they have a very close minimum focusing distance compared with a non-macro lens of the same focal length. Macro lenses also produce a 1:1 image, which means that the image quality when zoomed in will be greater than a non-macro lens, all things being equal. Macro lenses are typically more expensive than an equivalent prime lens of the same focal length. These lenses are best used when the camera is mounted on a tripod.

- **Tilt-shift lens -** An expensive and specialised type of lens used to "straighten" vertical surfaces such as buildings. They can also be used to create the "miniature" effect, making people and cityscapes look like ants! A tilt-shift lens is a fully manual lens type, and require time setting up to get a photo. These days, post-processing can achieve a reasonable approximation of the straightening effects of this lens.

As mentioned before, the suggestions below are for typical use. Don't be afraid to use the "wrong" lens for a situation, as it could produce unique and interesting photos. Plus, getting a photo is always better than not taking the photo because of the "wrong" lens.

# Wide-angle

A lens is typically considered to be wide-angle if it has a focal length of 24mm or less.

## Suggested uses

- Architecture
- Landscapes
- Narrow spaces
- Interiors
- Low light

## Limitations to consider for shooting

- **Compression -** Objects closer to the lens will appear disproportionately larger than background objects. A wide-angle lens is generally not a great choice for portraits of people, as facial features can appear out of proportion or distorted.

- **Barrel distortion -** This image distortion appears more typically on wide-angle lenses, where vertical and horizontal lines in image don't appear to be straight. This is generally correctable in post-processing, particularly for Raw files.

# Zoom

A zoom lens is the "typical" lens for a camera and is generally in the focal length range from 24 to 75mm.

## Suggested uses

- Everyday shooting
- Street photography

## Limitations to consider for shooting

- **Low light -** Most zoom lenses aren't great for low-light situations, particularly kit zoom lenses. This is because their widest aperture doesn't let too much light in, and so a slower shutter speed or higher ISO is required to get the shot in low-light situations.

- **Larger depth of field -** Building on the point above, the limited maximum aperture typically present on zoom lenses means that shots with a shallow depth of field (i.e. blurring out the background) are typically harder to achieve.

# Telephoto

A lens is typically considered to be telephoto if it has a focal length greater than 70mm.

## Suggested uses

- Sports
- Wild animals
- Distant objects
- Crowds (the compression of the image with make the crowd appear denser than reality)

## Limitations to consider for shooting

- **Weight** - Telephoto zooms, particularly those with a focal length of 200mm or above, tend to be very heavy.

- **Often not used** - Unless you are specifically shooting in situations that use a telephoto zoom (see above), the lens is often carried around all day and never leaves the bag.

- **Size** - Telephoto zoom lenses are big. Their size can sometimes be intimidating to others, including attracting extra attention from security.

# Prime

A prime lens has a fixed focal length and is typically made of higher quality optics for the price.

## Suggested uses

- Lowlight (typically the maximum aperture will be greater than a zoom)
- Capturing the sharpest image possible
- Portraits (for longer focal lengths)
- Macro photography

## Limitations to consider for shooting

- **Lack of flexibility** - Prime lenses don't provide as much flexibility in everyday situations as a zoom, and this may mean lost shots or frustration. If multiple focal lengths are desired, carrying several lenses can be much heavier over the course of a long day than a single zoom lens.

# FILTERS

As a group, filters are glass (or other transparent materials) that are screwed (or attached) to the lens to block specific (or all) wavelengths of light from hitting the camera's sensor. Filters include the following use cases:

## Polariser

Usually sold as a Circular Polarizer (CPL) filter, their function is to reduce glare and reflections from non-metallic surfaces. This can make bright skies and water more aesthetically pleasing, as well as providing greater transparency for objects hidden behind glass or under the water.

## Ultraviolet (UV)

In the days of film, a UV filter was required for sunny days and high altitudes to block UV rays from affecting the film in the camera. Modern digital cameras don't require such devices (despite what the person at the camera store tells you!). However, a UV filter also acts as protection for the front of your lens in the case of impact / scratching. Bear in mind that putting a low-quality UV filter on an expensive lens is going to degrade the quality of your pictures.

## Neutral Density (ND)

Used to darken exposure by reducing the amount of light that is let in to the camera's sensor. Think of an ND filter as the equivalent of putting sunglasses on your lens. ND filters make long exposure shots during daylight possible.

## Colour

Historically used for black and white film to block (or degrade) specific colours hitting the sensor. This effect can largely be replicated in post-production of Raw images.

# TRIPODS

Carrying a tripod around can be both the best thing, and the worst thing, for getting great images. A tripod will greatly improve your ability to capture sharp images, allow long exposure shots beyond what is feasible to manually hold a camera, and can also allow you to be in your shots without having to resort to taking a selfie. However, a tripod is also likely to be the heaviest item in your bag, it requires time and effort to set up and collapse, can make you feel self-conscious in public as it can attract attention, and can sometimes not be allowed to be used inside places such as places of worship and museums.

Having thought about the photos that you'd like to capture, consider if the following alternatives to a traditional tripod can achieve the same effect for you:

## Mini-tripod

Quite often you will be allowed to use a mini-tripod in places that a regular tripod is banned, simply because the mini-tripod doesn't create a trip hazard. Their lightness and size can mean that having a mini-tripod on hand gives you plenty of options without the need for a pack horse to carry your gear.

## Camera bag

Propping your camera on your camera bag can provide a degree of elevation, stability, and protection from the elements. In a pinch, the camera bag can prove much more versatile than you'd expect.

## Clothing (jacket, scarf, etc)

Similar to a camera bag, items of clothing that allow bunching up or being folded will enable you to nestle your camera in the right spot.

## Lens hood

The lens hood of your camera can be used to prop up the camera lens at an angle, allowing for getting that interior or architecture long exposure shot.

## Shelves / platforms / stable surfaces

Look for places that you can prop the camera, even if it means wedging the lens between objects such as holes in fences, to get that long exposure shot.

# MANAGING YOUR PHOTOS WHEN TRAVELING

Having an effective strategy for managing your photos during your travels may seem like paranoia to some, however most people agree that they'd rather lose their gear than lose their shots. A whole book can be dedicated to this topic alone, so here are some ideas and considerations. Professional photographers are much more likely to have additional requirements beyond what is suggested here, based on the value of their jobs, and the speed at which they need to deliver the product to the client.

# MEMORY CARDS

Memory cards are capable of storing more and more images and are becoming cheaper and cheaper over time. The simplicity of putting a 256Gb memory card in your camera and heading off on your trip has a certain appeal, as it is unlikely that you'll run out of space if you're just taking photos (shooting video is an entirely different proposition).

Consider the following when determining what size memory cards to carry:

## Carrying spares

Swapping memory cards can be a pain, particularly if you're right in the middle of the action and you run out of space. Nobody wants to be sitting there going through images to delete some to free up space! This means planning ahead and carrying spares.

## Memory card loss / corruption

If you were to lose your memory card, or it got corrupted (which can happen from time to time), how many images would you be prepared to lose? If your risk appetite is large, then this may not apply. Several smaller cards can provide you more protection than one huge card.

Smaller memory cards are typically cheaper than for one big card of the equivalent size. For example, 4x 16Gb cards will invariably be cheaper than one 64Gb card.

# LAPTOP / TABLET

Should you take your laptop or tablet with you on a travel photography trip? For many people, the thought of traveling anywhere without their full complement of toys is unthinkable. Your approach to carrying a laptop or tablet can depend on how long you're away for, weight considerations, relatively safety of where you're heading, and how much time you'll have to manage your photos. A few options to consider:

# Advantages of carrying a laptop and / or tablet

## Ease of backing up memory cards

This mostly applies to laptops, as they that have the ability to import data from a memory card. This data can then be copied onto a portable hard disk, or uploaded to a data storage service (DropBox, Google Drive, etc).

## Review your photos during your trip

We have discussed (page 29) the benefits of reviewing your own shots. Being able to take a look at the shots already taken when still on the ground can only enhance this concept. It allows you to respond more dynamically to any issues identified. The screen size of a laptop or tablet is superior to the LCD on the back of your camera. A quick recap of the benefits of review of your photos:

- **Feedback** - By reviewing the photos that you have already taken during the trip, you can understand what sort of photos you've been taking (e.g. predominantly architecture, wide-angle shots), and identify what type of photos that you want to add to your portfolio of the trip (e.g. more food, people, sunsets, cats, etc).

- **See what's missing** - Similar to the point above, going through your photos can help you identify locations that you haven't yet visited, or perhaps need to revisit to capture in different lighting conditions. This can complement your reviews of your photo shot list (page 75).

- **Technical issues** - This can include dust spots on your lens or camera sensor, a defect with your lens focusing, blurry photos in certain shooting conditions. Refer to the earlier section on tips to fix blurry photos (page 26).

## Post-processing

Travel can often include some periods of "enforced" downtime, such as flights, waiting in airports, middle of the day (harsh lighting conditions), or after dark when everybody has gone home. This can be a time to start working through the photos that you have taken and pick out your favourites, which can take more time than expected. Being able to get a jump-start on post-processing your photos whilst on the trip allows you to start sharing the images with family, friends, and social media. It also can further help as a review process of the photos you have been taking, and to identify photo opportunities that you might still need to seek out.

> **Tip:** Don't take on the task of post-processing to the exclusion of getting out and taking photos! Post-processing can sometimes become a black hole of time, and you suddenly discover that six hours have gone by and you've missed the best light of the day. You are on the ground for a limited amount of time, and the inside of a hotel room has limited photographic appeal.

## Downsides of traveling with a laptop / tablet

### Weight and space

A typical laptop, including its power supply, can easily weigh a couple of kilograms (five lbs), which can cumulatively add to the existing load that you are already carrying around. It is very sensible to carry your laptop (or tablet) in your carry-on baggage, along with your key camera equipment. This combination can very quickly tip the scales of the carry-on baggage allowance for most airlines.

### Airport security

Having to open your bags to take out a laptop or large tablet when going through airport security can add an extra few minutes to the airport experience. Not a huge deal, however it's worth noting here for completeness.

### Theft

Your laptop or tablet can make a tempting target for any would-be thief. If worried about theft, having travel insurance that covers the cost of your camera equipment as well as a laptop / tablet. You can carry your memory cards with you in a pocket, or in your camera bag with you.

# BACKUP STRATEGIES WHILST ON THE ROAD

Building on the points captured above about the use of laptops, here are some strategies that you can follow to help ensure that you don't lose any photos on your travel photography trip. Some of the ideas below may feel paranoid to you, and perhaps they are for your use case. However, consider the time and effort invested in your trip and how much more it would take to re-capture the same shots.

## Don't delete photos from memory cards

Up until you have had a chance to back up your memory cards, they are the only source of your photos and so should be protected. Don't delete photos from memory cards until you are home and have had the chance to take permanent copies.

## Copy from your memory card to each media

To provide a little extra protection against the chance of file corruption during the backup process, copy the files from the memory card to each of the backup media that you are using.

## More copies are generally better

By keeping more copies of your images, you are helping to manage the risk of file loss or corruption. This notion has to be balanced with a degree of pragmatism. There are diminishing returns for each incremental backup copy that you keep, particularly if each copy is subject to the same risks. In addition, unless you have a production company or huge corporate sponsor breathing down your neck, the cost and effort of multiple backups does need to be weighed up against the likelihood of having to go out and shoot the photos again. Most of the time, this will be possible, even if it's time-consuming and a bit more expensive.

## Physically separate your backups wherever possible

This is as much about the location of the copies as it is the number of copies. When traveling, it may not make much difference to have multiple versions of each image if they are all physically located in the same place. At a minimum, strive to have two copies of your images, one left in the safe in the hotel, the other carried with you. This can protect against accidental loss, theft, or corruption of a memory card.

If you have reasonable Internet access where you are staying, upload your photos to a cloud storage provider overnight, and then put your storage device back in the hotel safe when you're not in the room.

## Save to both memory cards at once

If your camera has two memory card slots (which is typically for higher-end cameras), you can save images to both cards simultaneously. Store the cards separately when you return to your hotel, including leaving one card in a safe and keeping the other card on you (if not in the camera).

## Laptop / tablet

Often the quickest and easiest place to back up to, your laptop (or tablet) can serve as a portable storage location. You can be limited by the amount of storage capacity of your laptop or tablet. In addition, tablets may import files in a different format than what you shot with or can downsize the files upon import. Consult the user manual for your tablet to understand how the tablet's operating system treats Raw (or JPEG) files upon import from a memory card.

A variant on this approach is to back up to your smartphone, which is invariably going to be with you. Many newer cameras have WiFi enabled, allowing you to copy images from the camera to your smartphone, or upload them to a cloud provider.

# Portable hard disk

This is the preferred solution to store backups when on the road. The cost of portable storage is very cheap, and the hard disk are compact and lightweight to carry. Bear in mind that hard disks contain moving parts and are relatively fragile. You can purchase portable hard disks with shock protection casing, however this shouldn't be relied upon to protect the disk. Treat any hard disk the same way that you would treat your laptop.

> **Tip:** Portable Solid State Drive (SSD) hard disks overcome the issue of moving parts, and are both faster and smaller than regular portable hard disks. However, they come with a hefty price tag.

# USB thumb drive

Similar to SSD drives, a USB thumb drive (or flash drive, pen drive, memory stick, etc) doesn't have any moving parts, and typically has fast copy speeds. This is especially true for USB 3.0, USB-C, and Thunderbolt devices. Capacities of these drives tend to be smaller, as their typical use case is for transferring smaller amounts of data.

The big advantage of a USB thumb drive over other physical storage options is that they can be put into your pocket. This allows you to carry a copy of your data (or at least the files not backed up elsewhere) on your person when out and about.

# Portable hard disk with an SD card slot

Some leading portable hard disk manufacturers have released hard disks with an SD card slot to streamline backup of your cards. This can be a lightweight, and less obtrusive, way to back up your memory cards compared with a laptop / tablet option. If your camera does not use SD cards, then this option won't apply.

# Cloud storage

This is the ideal long-term solution to be using for storage of your images. Reputable providers of cloud storage include DropBox, Google Drive, Amazon Drive, Microsoft

OneDrive, and many others. The advantages of these online storage solutions include:

- **Reliability** - The storage solutions employed by cloud providers mean that the likelihood of file corruption (once copied successfully) is negligible compared to using regular hard disk storage.

- **Redundancy** - The better cloud storage providers ensure that copies of your data are retained in multiple physical locations, even different parts of the world. This protects against localised risks such as natural disasters or fire.

- **Accessibility -** The ability to get to your photos, so long as you have an Internet connection, is a huge boon while you're traveling.

- **No weight** - Clouds don't weigh anything! In practical terms, you don't need to carry any physical storage devices.

- **Cost** - Perhaps this might be a little counter-intuitive, however the cost of ongoing storage may be quite minimal over time. In addition, you may be eligible for free storage data already if you use existing services such as Microsoft 365 (OneDrive) or Amazon Prime (Amazon Photos).

# RESOURCES

# GENERAL INFORMATION FOR TRAVEL PHOTOGRAPHY

## GLOSSARY

### Camera terms

Here is an overview of some of the camera terms that are mentioned in this guide:

#### Aperture

The opening of the lens, where light travels through. Often seen as synonymous with the iris / diaphragm, the aperture is the object that controls how much light is let through the lens onto the sensor.

In photography, aperture is usually denoted with respect to the focal length divided by the diameter of the opening of the lens. The bigger the denominator, the smaller the opening – e.g. f/1.4 is a much wider opening than f/16. This is why a "wider aperture" (e.g. f/1.4) is ideal for low-light situations, as the opening is larger thus letting in a greater amount of light.

#### Aperture Priority (A or Av on mode dial)

The aperture helps control the depth of field of an image. Selecting the Aperture Priority mode will allow you to manually select the desired aperture, and the camera will automatically select the shutter speed. Depending on your camera, the camera can automatically select the ISO as well.

#### Auto-bracketing

Your camera will have bracketing options that will automatically adjust the camera's exposure settings to take multiple images back-to-back. Settings can include choosing how many images to take, whether to shoot continuously (i.e. holding the shutter button down will take all of the photos in succession) or not, and how wide an exposure range to capture which is measured in "stops". A typical setting for auto-bracketing is "-2 stops", "normal", "+2 stops", often denoted in the camera as "-2,-,+2".

## Auto-ISO

Depending on which camera mode you are in, your camera will vary the ISO for a shot as part of getting the correct exposure. If the light is less than optimal, the camera will attempt to increase the ISO as its first priority. Bear this in mind if you are trying to get low-noise photos, as you may wish to consider changing the aperture setting instead.

## Auto Mode

The camera's metering and intelligence are used to determine the optimum exposure settings for the scene. Modern cameras will typically seek out reference objects such as faces to help determine what sort of scene it is shooting and expose accordingly.

## Back-button focusing

(This is an advanced approach). Back-button focusing involves de-coupling the camera's focusing mechanism from the shutter button; pushing the shutter button will then have no effect on the camera's focusing. Enabling back-button focusing will mean that your camera will no longer operate the way most people expect a camera to work (i.e. point and shoot). You will have much more control of what will be in focus for a shot, however you will need to separately focus the image before taking the shot.

The "back button" refers to the button(s) on the back of the camera that can be set to do spot focusing or tracking focusing. Using back button focusing means that your camera will focus predictably regardless of changes in the scene in front of you (e.g. the focus won't suddenly latch onto a different object when you push the shutter button). It takes practice to be comfortable with this technique, so allow time to come to terms with it.

## Cable release

This is a bit of a fancy term for a device that can be connected to your camera to allow you to take photos without having to touch the camera physically. This avoids you accidentally introducing shake into the camera. An alternative to a cable is to use a remote control release which uses Infrared (IR) to send a signal to the camera to take the photo.

For some modern cameras with BlueTooth or WiFi connectivity, the function of a cable release can be performed remotely via your smartphone.

## Continuous mode

Most cameras have the ability to shoot in a short burst mode, where multiple photos can be taken each second (measured in frames per second, or fps). You don't necessarily need to use the highest fps setting on your camera, however taking multiple shots at once increases your chances of one of the photos being sharp.

## Crop Factor (CF)

The CF rating of a camera is a measure of the dimensions of a camera's sensor with respect to a reference size. In the case of photography, the "full frame" reference size is a 35mm frame (replicating film). For example, a full frame with an aspect ratio of 3:2 might have a sensor size of 60mm x 40mm. A 1.5x crop factor sensor with the same 3:2 aspect ratio would have a sensor size of 40mm x 27mm. When comparing lenses, a 50mm lens for the full frame sensor would cover the same focal distance as a 75mm lens for the 1.5x crop factor sensor camera.

## Depth of Field (DoF)

This is a measure of the distance of objects from the plane of focus (i.e. where the lens is focused) that would be considered to be "sharp". As the depth of field increases, more objects in front and behind the plane of focus will be considered sharp. Conversely, a shallow depth of field means that objects will need to be very close to the plane of focus in order to be considered sharp.

A greater depth of field is generally preferred for landscape photos to capture in sharp focus objects in the near ground through to the far distance. A shallow depth of field is often desirable for portrait photos, to blur out the background of the photo.

## EXIF

The Exchangeable Image file Format (EXIF) is a standard used for embedding information related to an image as data that can be subsequently viewed either on the camera, or on a computer. This can include the exposure information from the camera (shutter speed, aperture, ISO), lens data, GPS data (if available), timestamp, and other camera data.

## Exposure

In simple terms, the amount of light that reaches the sensor in the camera. This is influenced by three factors in the camera that work in concert: the shutter speed, the aperture of the lens, and the ISO of the sensor.

## Exposure compensation

This adjusts the amount of light that is allowed into the camera through changing of one of the variables that affect exposure (see above). Knowing how your camera allows you to adjust exposure in each camera mode is key, and you may be able to adjust these settings in your camera's menu system.

## Focal length

In simplistic terms, the focal length refers to the combination of optical magnification and angle of view of a lens. A short focal length (e.g. 11mm) translates to a smaller amount of magnification and wider angle of view. Compare this with a longer focal length (e.g. 200mm) which has a greater optical magnification but a very small angle of view.

## Focus mode

Modern cameras have several focusing modes that can be used, utilising a combination of the information detected by the camera's sensor and intelligence in the camera's software to determine what the camera should focus on. This is what auto-focus modes tend to do, and mostly this works.

If you are wanting to be more precise about what is of greatest interest (i.e. greatest focus), you can use spot-metering to focus on what is in the middle of the camera's viewfinder. Understanding the radius that the spot focusing will cover is useful, so that you've got the right subject in frame when focusing.

For the most precise focus, switch your camera (and lens in many cases) to "manual focus" mode. Use the magnification preview feature of the camera to electronically zoom in (through the viewfinder or LCD) on what you want to focus in so ensure you get the tightest focus possible.

## Focus tracking

This can be a complex concept to master, particularly understanding how your camera will follow a moving object. In addition, understanding the limitations of focus tracking is important, including how much of the camera's frame can be used for focus-tracking. Stand-in moving objects to practice focus tracking can include young children, pets, and passing cars in the street.

## Full Frame (FF)

A camera sensor with a sensor size mimicking the traditional 35mm film format. As the sensor size increases, so do the manufacturing costs, hence FF cameras typically being more expensive. All things being equal, the larger sensor size will produce images with less noise.

## High Dynamic Range (HDR)

The human eye is capable of seeing a wider range of light than any camera in existence today. A simple way to visualise this is to think of a scene where you are standing in front of the inside window of a dark house, on a sunny day. A human eye can see definition in the shadows under the window as well as the brightly lit scenery outside of the window. Cameras will struggle with getting all of this detail without blowing the highlights (brightest parts of the image) or not capturing enough definition in the shadows.

HDR photographs look to overcome this camera limitation by combining multiple exposures of the same image, with each exposure taking in a difference range of light (normal, the bright areas, and the dark areas). These images can be then used to create a final image that better resembles that dynamic range that your eyes can see. Taken to extreme, these images can produce a cartoonish rendition of reality.

## Histogram

A histogram is a graphical representation of the spread of luminance (similar to brightness) across an image, from the shadows (on the left) to the highlights (on the right). The histogram is incredibly useful in determining whether an image is correctly exposed from a technical standpoint. You may wish to introduce some artistic flair into the photo, making it naturally over- or under-exposed depending on the situation (e.g. silhouettes against sunset).

# ISO

International Organization for Standardization (ISO). In camera terminology, this refers to how sensitive the sensor (or film in the old days) is to light. The higher the ISO number, the greater the sensitivity. However, greater sensitivity comes with greater noise (random coloured pixels).

The higher the ISO, the "noisier" the image. Depending on the situation, and the published size of the image, this may or may not be an issue. If you are shooting for thumbnails, or small-size web images / Instagram, then you are likely to have a fairly high tolerance for noise as it won't be visible in small images. However, if you're a "pixel peeper" (zooming in to every part of the image to look at quality), you are much more likely to seek out low-ISO images.

Understanding the maximum acceptable ISO of an image before noise becomes intolerable (a very subjective point) is important to enable you to get pleasing shots in low-light conditions. Noise is most apparent in dark areas / shadows, so practice shooting indoors or times when noise is mostly going to show up. For most cameras, shooting up to ISO 1600 will produce very acceptable images, and the bigger the camera's sensor, generally the higher the ISO that will be acceptable. For modern full frame cameras, images shot at up to ISO 6400 (or even beyond) are generally acceptable quality even when zoomed in. High ISO on phone cameras tends to be incredibly noisy (due to small camera sensor size) and is likely to be an option of last resort for most people.

# JPEG

Joint Photographic Experts Group, an industry standard for encoding and compressing images. Using the JPEG standard, the camera will automatically determine the optimum settings it thinks are best for the image and save them as part of the image capture process. This is considered a "destructive" process by virtue that applying the optimum settings (e.g. contrast, brightness, sharpness, etc) to the image will mean that the original image (as the camera's sensor captured it i.e. the Raw image) will be lost.

# Lens hood

A correctly fitted (i.e. facing "forward") lens hood serves two purposes, a) it shields the lens from light coming in from oblique angles therefore reducing the likelihood of unwanted lens flare, b) it's a cheap and very effective way of protecting the front of the lens from all sorts of casual knocks and scrapes.

Given that the lens hood is always attached to the lens when in use, it can be detached and used as an impromptu lens support for long exposure photos.

# Manual mode (M on mode dial)

The Manual mode of the camera allows you to select the aperture and the shutter speed of the camera. Depending on camera type, the camera can automatically select the ISO as well. This gives you maximum control over the exposure that you want for your image.

## Neutral Density (ND) filter

A ND filter blocks the amount of light passing through the lens, making the image darker for the same exposure settings (shutter speed, aperture, ISO). This can allow for effects such as a long exposure photo during daytime hours, as well as being able to photograph very bright objects.

## Noise

In simple terms, noise is unwanted image artefacts that occur principally when the image is taken. Noise is created by several factors, all which are quite complex physics phenomena. These include the effects of temperature of the sensor, signal amplification (how the sensor determines the "signal" of the image from background noise), the analogue-to-digital conversion process (reading the sensor and converting it into an image file), and what is termed shot noise (related to light sensitivity), as well as other causes.

## Noise reduction

Your camera can do all sorts of digital trickery to try to remove noise from images. In addition to changing the ISO settings (discussed above), noise reduction often involves taking multiple images in very quick succession. The camera's software will then average the pixels in these photos to smooth out the effect of random noise. Note that this feature in a camera is typically only applied to JPEG files as it is technically a form of post-processing.

Another way that a camera will look to remove noise for long exposure photos (usually with a shutter speed over one second) is to close the mirror and viewfinder, and then take an additional "black" image of the closed shutter (i.e. no image). The black image helps provide a baseline for noisy pixels on the sensor, typically caused by heat. The two images are combined, and this simple treatment is applied to the final image that is saved and is a process that can be applied to Raw files as well as JPEG.

## PASM

A reference to the mode dial on the camera, which includes the Program, Aperture priority, Shutter priority, and Manual modes.

## Plane of focus

The distance from the camera's sensor to the point that is most in focus. In simple terms it can be considered a plane (i.e. flat), however in reality it is a concave sphere. To visualise what this looks like, imagine a piece of string that is attached to the camera's sensor and pulled taut. Anywhere that the other end of the string touches will be part of the plane of focus.

## Polarizing Filter

Reduces glare and reflections off shiny surfaces such as water and glass. Objects behind the reflection (e.g. under the water, behind the glass) become more visible.

## Prime lens

A lens with a fixed focal length. Prime lenses typically have a wider maximum aperture (termed "faster") which can provide a shallower depth of field as well as increased exposure options in low-light situations. In addition, prime lenses typically come with higher quality lens glass which produce sharper images.

## Program mode (P on mode dial)

The camera automatically selects the aperture, shutter speed, and potentially the ISO as well. This differs from Auto mode as the camera won't attempt any fancy trickery to improve the photo beyond getting what it deems to be a correct exposure.

## Raw

The photography industry term for the image file that the camera saves, with no in-camera editing. Think of it as a digital negative, or the same as the film as it comes out of the camera (for those that remember film).

## Shutter Priority (S or Tv on mode dial)

Using the Shutter Priority mode, you select the shutter speed, and the camera selects the aperture. Depending on camera type, the camera can automatically select the ISO as well.

## Shutter speed

A measurement of how long the camera's sensor is exposed to light. A shutter speed can be adjusted to change exposure (along with aperture and / or ISO). The shutter speed can also be adjusted to capture the duration of an event / action. A longer shutter speed renders motion blur in images, which can be quite pleasing for photographing some objects such as water.

## Stop

In photographic terms, a stop is a reference to the relative change of light from a reference point. A decrease of one stop will halve the amount of light that hits the camera's sensor. Similarly, an increase of one stop will double the amount of light that hits the camera's sensor. Assuming that the shutter speed and ISO don't change (and the light source is constant), a change of aperture of one stop, from $f/5.6$ to $f/8$ will halve the amount of light let into the camera. Standard camera lens convention for measurement of aperture stops is based on a sequence of powers of the square root of two (the Inverse Square law in physics) that ranges from $f/1$, $f/1.4$, $f/2$, $f/2.8$, $f/4$, $f/5.6$, $f/8$, $f/11$, $f/16$, $f/22$, and $f/32$.

## Time lapse

Taking a series of photos at intervals is a great way to show the passage of time. Bear in mind that the more images that are taken, the bigger the drain on the camera's battery. Also think about the rate of change of whatever you're photographing – clouds don't vary much from one second to the next, however they do change minute to minute.

If you are able to control the location of the camera, you could create a time lapse that spans days / weeks / seasons. Technically this isn't using the time lapse functionality, rather returning to the same location at different times to take the photo.

## Tripod

A three-legged mount for supporting your camera and lens (page 52).

## Ultraviolet (UV) filter

Historically used to block UV rays from old film, however modern digital sensors are largely unaffected by UV rays. Their secondary use (apart from money makers from camera stores!) is to provide some degree of protection to the front of the lens from knocks / scrapes.

## Viewfinder

This term typically refers to the viewing device at the top of the camera that shows you the image that the camera can take. DSLR cameras tend to have Optical Viewfinders (OVF), although Sony has been leading the charge in the migration to Electronic Viewfinders (EVF). The advantage of an EVF is that it can show you the image that your camera will capture, even allowing for exposure compensation. Whereas, an OVF is essentially a window, showing you what your eye would normally see.

## White balance

White balance refers to adjusting the image so that different colours are all captured correctly. Many artificial light sources (e.g. fluorescent bulbs, tungsten bulbs) do not emit the full spectrum of light, and hence objects illuminated by these light sources are "missing" colours.

Adjusting the white balance will produce images in the same colour palette as what your eyes will see, as eyes are very good at compensating for different lighting conditions. If you are shooting in Raw, the white balance that you set in the camera will have zero effect on the Raw image. However, if you are shooting in JPEG, the camera may not always select the correct white balance, leaving your photos either looking very blue or very yellow.

Cameras will have suggested white balance settings to take advantage of typical indoor and outdoor light conditions. If you are shooting a scene with multiple different sources of light (e.g. sun and fluorescent light), it might be easier to shoot in Raw and adjust the white balance to a good compromise in post-processing.

# Non-camera terms

## Airline reward program

Most major airlines (and even some budget ones) want to be able to provide a premium experience for loyal customers. For the airline industry, Economy class passengers are the least financially rewarding group as this type of customer typically flies infrequently and shops based on price. However, business travellers and those that enjoy travel / flying are the market that airline reward programs want to tap into. Rewards range widely from free / discount upgrades, airport lounge access, fast track for airport check-in and airport security check-in, and extra baggage allowance.

## Bucket list

This idiom stems from the phrase "to kick the bucket", a rather crude way of describing somebody's death (the origins of the expression have been lost in history). A bucket list typically includes activities / events that you'd like to achieve before dying. As it relates to travel, paradoxically the more you travel, the more that this list is likely to grow rather than shrink; you will be inspired to see more and more places. You have been warned!

## Frequent Flyer (FF)

A generic term that can be used to describe somebody that flies on a regular basis. However, it usually applies to somebody who is looking to acquire frequent flyer miles and / or improve their "status" with an airline (see "Airline reward program").

## IATA

International Air Transport Association (IATA), an airline trade association. Three-digit IATA codes are associated with airports around the world and are used to denote destinations e.g. HKG is Hong Kong's, MAD is Madrid's Adolfo Suárez airport.

# BOOKING TRAVEL

Planning your next trip? Avoid the hassle of looking for your much-needed information all over the Internet. We have gathered all of these resources for your convenience.

# AGGREGATORS AND REWARDS POINTS

These are online equivalents to supermarkets for hotel and flight options. The sites listed below are well-established within the industry.

## Hotel accommodation aggregators

Find the best hotel accommodation based on factors such as location, price, deals, etc. Each of them has their own customer loyalty program that offers discounts and bonuses.

### Hotels.com
https://www.hotels.com

They have tie-ups in more than 200 countries and territories, and they have 90 global websites that support 41 languages. They also accept a wide range of currencies for payments. Note: Parent company is Expedia.

### Expedia
https://www.expedia.com

Expedia has a flight and hotel bundle and they offer holiday rentals and cruises. However, they accept limited types of currency for payments.

### LastMinute
https://www.lastminute.com

Aside from hotel and flight accommodation, LastMinute has an Inspire Me page that gives visitors holiday ideas if they are looking for one. All you need to do is pick the perfect holiday that you have in mind, the date you want, and the budget you have. The only downside – it's exclusive for United Kingdom residents but except for that, their other services are available internationally.

### Kayak
https://www.kayak.com

Kayak enables you to compare prices with other travel sites simultaneously, allowing you to pick the best price according to your budget or schedule. For those planning a group holiday, their "Trip Huddle" feature enables you to pick the perfect holiday getaway and plan your trip easily.

## Agoda

https://www.agoda.com

Agoda allows you to filter your searches based on price, rating, and proximity of the area to the nearest landmarks and areas of interest, giving you an idea what you're getting based on your preferences. Clicking the "Secret Deals" option allows you to see hotels offering huge discounts – you just have to be fast to grab them.

## Booking

https://www.booking.com

Similar functionality to the other aggregators (above). If you indicate that you're traveling for business, it gives you different search filters based on what a businessperson might need, such as WiFi and parking. It also supports a wide range of languages and currencies.

# Non-hotel accommodation aggregators

If you'd rather stay in a house owned by a local in your planned destinations, these are some of the sites you can check out for good deals:

## AirBnB

https://www.airbnb.com

The eponymous AirBnB has revolutionised the accommodation market, shaking up the hotel industry and providing a range of private accommodation options previously unavailable to travellers. If you expect AirBnB to be offering only accommodation, you'll be pleasantly surprised. They are now also offering activities led by local hosts, from cooking classes to an educational experience with a marine biologist.

## Home Away

https://www.homeaway.com

Home Away might not be as popular as AirBnB but this site has more than 2 million properties listed in over 190 countries. It also supports a wide range of currencies from the Argentine Peso to Vietnamese Dong.

## Homestay

https://www.homestay.com

If you are travelling on a budget and want cheaper yet comfortable accommodation, Home Stay is an ideal alternative. The site is a good place to start, especially for solo travellers.

## Staydu

https://www.staydu.com

This site can be considered innovative because some of the local hosts allow you to stay for free in exchange for "help," which can be language learning, housework, farm work, etc.

### Couch Surfing
https://www.couchsurfing.com/

Very much the home stay option, this may or may not be an ideal fit for somebody traveling with the intent of taking photos. Cheap and cheerful, and a great way to meet locals.

## Flight aggregators

### Google Flights
https://www.google.com/flights/

What's best about Google Flights is that it shows the cheapest price when you hover over the dates on the calendar. It also allows you to choose how many stopovers you would prefer for your flight.

### Skyscanner
https://www.skyscanner.net

Skyscanner lets you find great deals, cheap tickets, and even last-minute flights anywhere in the world. It also has travel guides to some of the major cities in the world. If you are looking for flights with airlines with a specific airline group (e.g. OneWorld, Star Alliance, Sky Team, etc), you can filter for this.

### Hipmunk
https://www.hipmunk.com

Hipmunk's interface is simple and straightforward. If you tick the "price graph" option, it will give you a list of the cheapest flights for the next 90 days.

### Momondo
https://global.momondo.com

Momondo is a new player in the travel niche; thus, it strives to please visitors by giving them good flight deals. When you sign-up, the three latest searches you made will appear right on the homepage making it easier to track them.

## Rewards points utilisation

Travel expenses can quickly accumulate, so it makes sense to take advantage of savings whenever you can. Know where and how to get awesome redemption rates, complimentary perks, and other benefits from airlines and airline groups.

### God Save The Points
https://www.godsavethepoints.com

This UK-focused site offers a lot of insights not only about discounts and rewards but also credit card advice. They also connect with hundreds of local bloggers who provide insider insights from all over the world. If you are a newbie traveller, no worries because they give you tons of advice and tips as well.

## The Points Guy
https://www.thepointsguy.com

Maximise your travel – that is what The Points Guy is all about. Not only does it give you the best deals and tips how to utilise your points, it also gives you the latest travel-related news. More so, it also has useful tips for families from credit cards to driving around a certain city.

## Flyer Talk
https://www.flyertalk.com

Flyer Talk has a vast and active community that regularly posts and discusses anything about travel, especially rewards, discounts, miles, and more. They also have the "Lounge Connect" and "Flight Connect" features which allow you to meet up with fellow travellers.

## Rewards Expert
https://www.rewardsexpert.com

The site helps you find and use the credit card that will give you the best deals, find the most convenient flights for less miles, have the best rebates when shopping. It even has information on what airport has the best food. So next time you have a long layover anywhere in the world, you'll know what food to expect in that particular airport.

## Frugal Travel Guy
https://www.frugaltravelguy.com

Don't you just love it if you discover that your rewards card allows you to book an airport pickup? That's just one of the helpful tips you can get from this site's treasure trove of information.

## Million Mile Secrets
https://www.millionmilesecrets.com

Hot deals, reviews, tips, guides – these are some of the things you can get from Million Mile Secrets. But there's more to this site, such as booking some of the best attractions in the world for free, minus the long lines.

# NATIONAL TRAIN NETWORKS

The following are the English-language websites for the major train networks that operate in countries where cross-country train travel is a generally viable option. Whilst train networks exist in other countries, they are not a usual form of transport for long distances (e.g Australia).

## Americas

### Canada

Via Rail - https://www.viarail.ca/en

### United States

Amtrak - https://www.amtrak.com/home.html

## Asia

### China

China Railway - http://www.china-railway.com.cn/en/

### Hong Kong

Mass Transit Railway - http://www.mtr.com.hk/en/customer/tourist/index.php

### India

Indian Railways - http://www.indianrailways.gov.in

### Japan

East Japan Railway Company (JR East) - https://www.jreast.co.jp/e/

Central Japan Railway Company (JR Central) - https://global.jr-central.co.jp/en/

West Japan Railway Company (JR West) - https://www.westjr.co.jp/global/en/

Hokkaido Railway Company (JR Hokkaido) - http://www2.jrhokkaido.co.jp/global/

Kyushu Railway Company (JR Kyushu) - http://www.jrkyushu.co.jp/english/

Shikoku Railway Company (JR Shikoku) - http://www.jr-shikoku.co.jp/global/en/

Japan Rail Pass - http://www.japanrailpass.net/en/

## Malaysia

Keretapi Tanah Malaysia (KTM) - https://www.ktmb.com.my/

## Singapore

Singapore Mass Rapid Transport (SMRT) - https://www.smrttrains.com.sg/

## South Korea

Korail - http://info.korail.com/mbs/english/

## Taiwan

Taiwan Railways - https://www.railway.gov.tw/en/index.aspx

# Europe

## Pan-Europe

Interrail - https://www.interrail.eu/

## Austria

OBB (Austria Federal Railways - Österreichische Bundesbahnen) - https://www.oebb.at/en/

## Belgium

SNCB (Belgian National Railways - Société nationale des chemins de fer belges) - https://www.belgiantrain.be/en

## Bulgaria

BDZh (Bulgarian State Railways - Bălgarski Dărzhavni Zheleznitsi) - http://www.bdz.bg/en/

## Croatia

HŽ (Croatian Railways - Hrvatske željeznice) - http://www.hzpp.hr/en

## Czech Republic

ČD (Czech Railways - České dráhy) - https://www.cd.cz/en/default.htm

## Denmark

DSB (Danish State Railways - Danske Statsbaner) - https://www.dsb.dk/en

## Estonia

Eesti Raudtee (Estonian Railways) - http://www.evr.ee/en/

Elron - http://elron.ee/en/

## Finland

VR (VR Ltd - VR Oy) - https://www.vr.fi/cs/vr/en/frontpage

## France

SNCF (French National Railway Company - Société nationale des chemins de fer français) - https://www.sncf.com/en

## Germany

DB (German Railways - Deutsche Bahn) - https://www.deutschebahn.com/en

## Greece

TrainOSE - http://www.trainose.gr/en/

## Hungary

MAV (Hungarian State Railways - Magyar Államvasutak) - https://www.mavcsoport.hu/en

## Ireland

Iarnród Éireann (Irish Rail) - http://www.irishrail.ie/

## Italy

Ferrovie dello Stato Italiane (Italian State Railways) - https://www.trenitalia.com/tcom-en

## Latvia

Pasažieru vilciens - https://www.pv.lv/en/

# Lithuania

LG (Lithuanian Railways - Lietuvos geležinkeliai) - http://www.litrail.lt/en/home

# Luxembourg

CFL (Luxembourg Railways - Chemins de Fer Luxembourgeois) - http://www.cfl.lu/en/home

# Macedonia

MZ (Macedoniann Railways - Makedonski Železnici) - https://mzt.mk/?lang=en

# The Netherlands

NS (Dutch Railways - Nederlandse Spoorwegen) - https://www.ns.nl/en

# Norway

Norwegian State Railways - https://www.nsb.no/en/frontpage

# Poland

PKP (Polish State Railways - Polskie Koleje Państwowe) - http://www.pkp.pl/en/

# Portugal

CP (Portuguese Railways - Caminhos de ferro portugueses) - https://www.cp.pt/passageiros/en

# Romania

Căile Ferate Române (Romanian Railways) - https://www.cfrcalatori.ro/en/

# Russia

RZhD - (Russian Railways - Rossiskiye Zheleznye Dorogi) - https://pass.rzd.ru/main-pass/public/en

# Slovakia

ZSSK (Railways of the Slovak Republic - Železničná Spoločnosť Slovensko) - https://www.zsr.sk/pre-cestujucich/train-connections-elis/

## Slovenia

SZ (Slovenian Railways - Slovenske železnice) - https://www.slo-zeleznice.si/en/passenger-transport

## Spain

SpainRail - https://renfe.spainrail.com/

## Sweden

SJ (State Railways - Statens Järnvägar) - https://www.sj.se/en/home.html

## Switzerland

SBB (Swiss Federal Railways - Schweizerische Bundesbahnen) - https://www.sbb.ch/en/home.html

## United Kingdom

National Rail - http://www.nationalrail.co.uk/

# VISAS

## OPTIONS TO CONSIDER

### Visa-free / electronic visa / visa on arrival programs

Visa waiver programs enable passport holders of permitted countries to enter into a country without a visa for a short stay (generally between 30 to 90 days). Most visa waiver programs tend to apply two points to determination of which countries are eligible for a visa waiver. The first is that visa waivers are typically granted to so-called "developed" countries (European Union, Switzerland, Norway, Iceland, Monaco, Liechtenstein, United States, Canada, Singapore, Hong Kong, Japan, South Korea, Taiwan, Australia, and New Zealand) to have access to visa waivers. The second tenet, reciprocity, also does applies, with an expectation that countries afford each other similar access rights, which doesn't always work out!

### Stopover visas

Layovers can become inevitable as part of long-distance travel. Wouldn't it be great if you can spend your time exploring a city rather than sit at the airport lounge for 12 hours? Some of the countries listed in the summary by location section offer stopover visas for periods of 24 – 96 hours, for certain nationalities (separate to visa-free entry). Only countries that offer a stopover visa option are mentioned.

### Transiting

The definition of transit (from an immigration standpoint) does vary to a degree from country to country. In immigration terms, transit relates to a person either physically being present in a country (even if they haven't gone through immigration), or briefly entering the country (passing immigration) on their way to a third destination. This last way of thinking about transit is particularly relevant for cruise ship passengers, who are entering a country for a matter of hours before heading off somewhere else.

Within airports around the world, there is a concept of "non-sterile" vs "sterile" immigration, with the latter allowing passengers to change flights without having to go through any immigration process as they stay "air side" of the terminal. Some countries will insist on passengers of certain nationalities having a transit visa, even if they don't enter through the immigration of the country. This is quite common for the United States and Canada, as well as many European Union countries. On the other hand, countries such as Singapore operate a "sterile" immigration approach. As long as you stay on the "air side" of the airport (i.e. don't pass through immigration), you don't require a visa.

A rule of thumb for transiting through a country – if you would require a visa to actually enter the country, chances are that you'll need some form of visa / permission to transit.

# SUMMARY BY LOCATION

Below is an overview of the basic tourist visa requirements for many popular destinations for budding travel photographers. Note that immigration rules for countries change all the time, and often quite quickly. Ensure that you have the appropriate visa(s) in place before your travel, as you could be refused boarding onto a plane, or be refused entry into the country that was to be your destination.

## Americas

### Argentina

Government site - http://www.migraciones.gov.ar/accesible/indexA.php?visas (in Spanish)
Wikipedia - https://en.wikipedia.org/wiki/Visa_policy_of_Argentina

Holders of 87 jurisdictions can enter Argentina for up to 90 days, including all European Union countries and most countries in the Americas.

### Brazil

Government site - http://www.portalconsular.itamaraty.gov.br/vistos#precisa (in Portuguese, and some English)
Wikipedia - https://en.wikipedia.org/wiki/Visa_policy_of_Brazil

Citizens of Canada, Australia, and the United States all need a visa to enter Brazil. On the other hand, citizens of European Union, other countries in the Americas, and many Asian countries (including New Zealand) can enter for up to 90 days.

### Canada

Government site - http://www.cic.gc.ca/english/visit/visas.asp
Wikipedia - https://en.wikipedia.org/wiki/Visa_policy_of_Canada

For countries that are allowed visa-free entry, you will need to apply for an Electronic Travel Authorization (eTA) prior to travel to Canada. This includes many Northern American countries, European Union, Australia, New Zealand, and some Asian countries.

### Chile

Government site - https://serviciosconsulares.cl/tramites/visa-de-turismo-simple-o-multiple (in Spanish)
Wikipedia - https://en.wikipedia.org/wiki/Visa_policy_of_Chile

Chile allows 92 countries to stay without a visa for up to 90 days, including European Union, Americas, and many countries across Asia (including New Zealand). Australian passport holders entering Chile via Santiago International Airport are required to pay a "reciprocity fee" (currently USD 117).

## Colombia

Government site - https://www.cancilleria.gov.co/en/procedures_services/visa/requirements
Wikipedia - https://en.wikipedia.org/wiki/Visa_policy_of_Colombia
Colombia allows 101 countries to stay without a visa for a maximum of 90 days, including European Union, the Americas, and many countries across Asia (including Australia and New Zealand).

## Panama

Government site - https://www.embassyofpanama.org/visas-1/
Wikipedia - https://en.wikipedia.org/wiki/Visa_policy_of_Panama

Panama allows a large number of countries to visit visa-free, including European Union, most of the Americas, most Asian nations, and many African nations.

## United States

Government site - https://esta.cbp.dhs.gov/
Wikipedia - https://en.wikipedia.org/wiki/Visa_Waiver_Program

Citizens of 38 countries are eligible for the Visa Waiver Program, which requires them to apply for an Electronic System for Travel Authorization (ESTA) at least 72 hours before travel. The ESTA lasts for two years and can be used on multiple occasions. Eligible countries include the majority of the European Union and several Asian nations (including Australia and New Zealand).

# Asia

## Australia

Government site - https://www.australia.gov.au/help-and-contact/faqs/visas-and-immigration
Wikipedia - https://en.wikipedia.org/wiki/Visa_policy_of_Australia

For countries that are allowed visa-free entry, there are two options depending on your passport. For European Union and other Western European countries, you can get an eVisitor that allows stays of up to three months. The Electronic Travel Authority (ETA) is available for Brunei, Hong Kong, Japan, Malaysia, Singapore, South Korea, Canada, and United States citizens, and allows stays of up to three months.

Some nationalities require a transit visa if they are going to be transiting through Australian airport for greater than eight hours.

## Cambodia

Government site - https://www.evisa.gov.kh/
Wikipedia - https://en.wikipedia.org/wiki/Visa_policy_of_Cambodia

Citizens of countries that are members of ASEAN can stay 21 – 30 days visa-free in Cambodia. Citizens of Bulgaria and Hungary can stay visa-free up to 90 days; India and the South Korea are given 60 days while Peru, Iran, and China have a 30-day visa-free eligibility.

## China

Government site - https://www.visaforchina.org/CBR_EN/generalinformation/faq/275556.shtml
Wikipedia - https://en.wikipedia.org/wiki/Visa_policy_of_China

Passport holders of most countries require a visa to enter China. Some Eastern European, Caribbean, and African country citizens can enter visa-free for 30 days, and citizens of Brunei, Singapore, and Japan can enter for 15 days.

China has a transit visa policy in 18 cities that allow visitors from 53 countries to stay over for periods between 72 and 144 hours, based on a set number of conditions (refer to website for further details). Note that this is for countries that do not already have a visa-free eligibility. Countries with this stopover option include European Union, Canada, United States, as well as a number of Asian nations (including Australia, New Zealand, South Korea).

## Hong Kong

Government site - https://www.immd.gov.hk/eng/services/visas/visit-transit/visit-visa-entry-permit.html
Wikipedia - https://en.wikipedia.org/wiki/Visa_policy_of_Hong_Kong

Hong Kong has a visa-free entry policy for 170 countries, with the typical visa-free stay 90 days. This includes citizens of the European Union (except United Kingdom – 180 days), Western European nations, many Asian nations (including Australia and New Zealand), Canada, and the United States.

## India

Government site - https://mea.gov.in/bvwa.htm
Wikipedia - https://en.wikipedia.org/wiki/Visa_policy_of_India

India has an e-Visa program, Electronic Travel Authorisation (ETA), that once granted, allows entry for citizens of 113 countries for a period of 60 days.

It is possible to get a three-day transit visa for a single stopover or two short stops with a 15-day validity period. This transit visa needs to be obtained in advance, similar to the e-Visa.

# Indonesia

Government site - http://www.imigrasi.go.id/index.php/en/public-services/visit-visa
Wikipedia - https://en.wikipedia.org/wiki/Visa_policy_of_Indonesia

Citizens of 170 countries can obtain a 30-day visa on arrival, including citizens of the European Union, most Asian nations (including Australia and New Zealand), the majority of the Americas, and many African nations.

# Israel

Government site - https://mfa.gov.il/MFA/ConsularServices/Pages/Visas.aspx
Wikipedia - https://en.wikipedia.org/wiki/Visa_policy_of_Israel

Visa-free entry is available for 100 countries for stays up to 90 days, including citizens of the European Union, most Asian nations (including Australia and New Zealand), the majority of the Americas, and many African nations.

# Japan

Government site - https://www.mofa.go.jp/j_info/visit/visa/index.html
Wikipedia - https://en.wikipedia.org/wiki/Visa_policy_of_Japan

Japan has a visa waiver agreement with 66 countries with a maximum stay of 90 days. This includes European Union and other Western European countries, many Asian countries (including Brunei, Hong Kong, Singapore, South Korea, Taiwan, Thailand), and many countries from the Americas.

In addition, Japan offers a transit visa for some nationalities not eligible for visa waiver. This transit visa allows a stopover of up to 15 days for tourist purposes.

# Jordan

Government website - http://www.mota.gov.jo/contents/visa_information.aspx
Wikipedia - https://en.wikipedia.org/wiki/Visa_policy_of_Jordan

Jordan provides visa-free access to a number of Gulf states, and visa-on-arrival to a large number of countries. This includes European Union and European countries, the majority of the Americas, many Asian nations (including Australia, Brunei, China, Hong Kong, India, Indonesia, Japan, Malaysia, Singapore, South Korea, Taiwan, Thailand).

# Malaysia

Government website - https://www.imi.gov.my/index.php/en/visa/visa-requirement-by-country.html
Wikipedia - https://en.wikipedia.org/wiki/Visa_policy_of_Malaysia

Malaysia grants 90-day visa-free entry to 63 countries including European Union countries and Western Europe, several Asian nations (including Australia, Japan, New Zealand, South

Korea), most of the Americas, many Middle Eastern nations. In addition, 30-day visa-free entry is available to a further 97 countries.

Malaysia offers a Transit Without Visa (TWOV) option for up to 120 hours stopover for several Asian nations that would ordinarily require a visa. This covers nationals of Bangladesh, Bhutan, China India, Myanmar, Nepal, Pakistan, Sri Lanka, and Vietnam.

## New Zealand

Government website - https://www.immigration.govt.nz/new-zealand-visas/apply-for-a-visa/tools-and-information/general-information/visa-waiver-countries
Wikipedia - https://en.wikipedia.org/wiki/Visa_policy_of_New_Zealand

New Zealand allows 60 countries visa-free entry for up to 90 days stay, including the European Union (180 days for United Kingdom), several countries of the Americas, many Asian nations (Brunei, Hong Kong, Japan, Malaysia Singapore, South Korea, Taiwan).

## Philippines

Government website - https://www.dfa.gov.ph/guidelines-requirements
Wikipedia - https://en.wikipedia.org/wiki/Visa_policy_of_the_Philippines

The Philippines operates a flexible visa-free process, allowing citizens of a large number of countries to enter the country for up to 30 days visa-free. This includes the European Union, the Americas, most Asian nations, as well as many Middle Eastern and African nations.

## Qatar

Government website - https://portal.moi.gov.qa/wps/portal/MOIInternet/services/inquiries/visaservices
Wikipedia - https://en.wikipedia.org/wiki/Visa_policy_of_Qatar

Qatar offers visa-free entry to 80 countries with a maximum stay of 30 – 90 days, depending on citizenship. European Union (excluding Ireland and United Kingdom), Western European nations, and some Caribbean nations can stay for 90 days. Many countries in the Americas, several Asian nations (including Australia and New Zealand), can stay for 30 days.

Qatar has introduced transit visa for passengers of any nationality for periods up to 96 hours, when traveling on Qatar Airways through Hamad International Airport.

## Singapore

Government website - https://www1.mfa.gov.sg/Services/Visitors/Visa-Information
Wikipedia - https://en.wikipedia.org/wiki/Visa_policy_of_Singapore

Singapore has visa-free access to a number of countries, including European Union, Australia, New Zealand, Norway, South Korea, Switzerland, and United States Citizens being able to stay for up to 90 days. Most other nations can stay for up to 30 days.

Singapore operates a Visa Free Transit Facility (VFTF) for nationals of several countries that would otherwise require a visa to enter Singapore, including India and several former Soviet states. This allows the traveller to enter Singapore for up to 96 hours.

## South Korea

Government website - http://english.visitkorea.or.kr/enu/TRV/TV_ENG_2_1.jsp
Wikipedia - https://en.wikipedia.org/wiki/Visa_policy_of_South_Korea

South Korea has visa waiver agreements in place for 117 countries, for periods generally up to 90 days. This includes European Union and other Western European nations, many Asian nations (including Brunei, Hong Kong, Macau, Singapore, South Korea, Taiwan, Thailand), and many countries from the Americas.

## Taiwan

Government website - https://www.boca.gov.tw/np-137-2.html
Wikipedia - https://en.wikipedia.org/wiki/Visa_policy_of_Taiwan

Taiwan gives visa-free access for 90 days to 54 countries including European Union, Canada, United States, some Asian nations (Australia, Japan, New Zealand, South Korea). A visa-free stay for 30 days is available for many Caribbean nations as well as Singapore.

## Thailand

Government website - http://www.mfa.go.th/main/en/services/4908
Wikipedia - https://en.wikipedia.org/wiki/Visa_policy_of_Thailand

Thailand's visa exemption program allows tourists from 55 countries to visit Thailand without a visa for a period between 30-90 days. Countries granted visa-free entry include most European nations, Canada, United States, many Asian nations (including Australia, Japan, Malaysia, Philippines, Singapore).

## Turkey

Government website - http://www.mfa.gov.tr/visa-information-for-foreigners.en.mfa
Wikipedia - https://en.wikipedia.org/wiki/Visa_policy_of_Turkey

Turkey allows 78 countries to enter the country visa-free for 90 days, including most European nations, most of the Americas (excluding Canada and United States), many Asian nations (including Hong Kong, Japan, Malaysia, New Zealand, Singapore, South Korea). Citizens of United Kingdom, Australia, Canada, and United States require a visa.

## United Arab Emirates

Government website - https://www.government.ae/en/information-and-services/visa-and-emirates-id
Wikipedia - https://en.wikipedia.org/wiki/Visa_policy_of_the_United_Arab_Emirates

There are 47 countries that are granted visa-free entry in to the United Arab Emirates, including European Union countries (except Ireland and United Kingdom), some Western European countries, and some countries of the Americas. Citizens of Australia, Canada, Hong Kong, Malaysia, New Zealand, Singapore, South Korea, United Kingdom, and United States need to obtain a free visa on arrival for a 30 day stay.

Citizens of most countries can obtain a transit visa to stay up to 96 hours, and it is free for the first 48 hours.

## Vietnam

Government website - https://vietnamvisa.govt.vn/vietnam-visa/government-policies/
Wikipedia - https://en.wikipedia.org/wiki/Visa_policy_of_Vietnam

Vietnam allows 24 countries to enter visa-free for a duration of between 14 to 90 days, including citizens of Cambodia, Indonesia, Malaysia, Philippines, Singapore, Thailand, Denmark, Finland, France, Germany, Italy, Japan, Norway, Russia, South Korea, Spain, Sweden, United Kingdom.

# Europe

As a basic tenet of European Union membership, member states allow citizens of each country to move seamlessly between each country's borders, with few exceptions. Therefore, holders of a European Union country passport can travel indefinitely to each European Union country (and so are not mentioned below).

## Schengen area

Government website - https://ec.europa.eu/home-affairs/what-we-do/policies/borders-and-visas/visa-policy/schengen_visa_en
Wikipedia - https://en.wikipedia.org/wiki/Visa_policy_of_the_Schengen_Area

Members of the Schengen states have similar visa policies (unless stated) for visa-free entry. Schengen state members, all European Union citizens, and Switzerland have freedom of movement between Schengen states. The Schengen states are:

- Austria
- Belgium
- Czech Republic
- Denmark (excluding Faroe Islands and Greenland)
- Estonia
- Finland
- France (excluding overseas territories)
- Germany
- Greece
- Hungary
- Iceland
- Italy

- Latvia
- Liechtenstein
- Lithuania
- Luxembourg
- Malta
- Netherlands (excluding Caribbean territories)
- Norway (excluding Svalbard)
- Poland
- Portugal
- Slovakia
- Slovenia
- Spain
- Sweden
- Switzerland

Citizens of 62 countries have visa-free access to the Schengen area for up to 90 days, including the majority of the Americas, as well as many Asian nations (Australia, Brunei, Hong Kong, Japan, Malaysia, New Zealand, Singapore, South Korea, Taiwan).

## Bulgaria

Government website - https://www.mfa.bg/en/services-travel/consular-services/travel-bulgaria/visa-bulgaria

Although not yet part of the Schengen area, Bulgaria applies the same visa-free entry as per the Schengen area.

## Croatia

Government website - http://www.mvep.hr/en/consular-information/visas/visa-requirements-overview/

Although not yet part of the Schengen area, Croatia applies the same visa-free entry as per the Schengen area.

## Cyprus

Government website - http://www.mfa.gov.cy/mfa/mfa2016.nsf/mfa81_en/mfa81_en?OpenDocument

Cyprus applies the same visa-free entry as per Schengen area. Note that this does not apply to Northern Cyprus, which is treated separately for immigration purposes.

## Ireland

Government website - http://www.inis.gov.ie/en/INIS/Pages/visa-required-countries
Wikipedia - https://en.wikipedia.org/wiki/Visa_policy_of_Ireland

European Union citizens can enter Ireland without restriction. In addition, citizens of 56 other countries can enter Ireland visa-free, including most of the Americas, many Asian nations (Australia, Brunei, Hong Kong, Japan, Malaysia, New Zealand, Singapore, South Korea, Taiwan).

## Macedonia

Government website - http://www.mfa.gov.mk/index.php?option=com_content&view=article&id=222&Itemid=661&lang=en
Wikipedia - https://en.wikipedia.org/wiki/Visa_policy_of_the_Republic_of_Macedonia

Macedonia allows visa-free entry to a number of countries for up to 90 days, including European Union, the Americas, many Asian nations (Australia, Brunei, Hong Kong, Japan, Malaysia, New Zealand, Singapore, South Korea, Taiwan).

## Romania

Government website - https://www.mae.ro/en/node/2035

Although not yet part of the Schengen area, Romania applies the same visa-free entry as per the Schengen area.

## Russia

Government website - http://www.mid.ru/en/migration_registration
Wikipedia - https://en.wikipedia.org/wiki/Visa_policy_of_Russia

Citizens of many of the former Soviet states are entitled to visa-free access to Russia for up to 90 days. In addition, many South American and Asian nations (including South Korea, Thailand, Brunei, and Hong Kong) are eligible for visa-free entry for periods ranging from 14-90 days.

## United Kingdom

Government website - https://www.gov.uk/browse/visas-immigration
Wikipedia - https://en.wikipedia.org/wiki/Visa_policy_of_the_United_Kingdom

The United Kingdom offers visa-free access to 56 countries for up to six months. This covers most of the Americas, as well as many countries in Asia (Australia, Brunei, Hong Kong, Japan, Malaysia, New Zealand, Singapore, South Korea, Taiwan).

# Africa

## Botswana

Government website - http://www.gov.bw/Ministries--Authorities/Ministries/Ministry-of-Labour--Home-Affairs-MLHA/Tools--Services/Services--Forms/Requirements-for-VISA-application/
Wikipedia - https://en.wikipedia.org/wiki/Visa_policy_of_Botswana

Botswana provides visa-free entry for 103 countries for up to 90 days at a time. This includes European Union (and other European nations), the Americas, as well as many Asian nations (Australia, Brunei, Hong Kong, Japan, Malaysia, New Zealand, Singapore, South Korea).

## Egypt

Government website - https://www.visa2egypt.gov.eg/eVisa/
Wikipedia - https://en.wikipedia.org/wiki/Visa_policy_of_Egypt

Egypt offers visa-free access to a limited number of countries (such as Hong Kong and Malaysia), and visa on arrival for European Union, Australia, Canada, Japan, New Zealand, Norway, South Korea, and United States.

## Kenya

Government website - http://evisa.go.ke/evisa.html
Wikipedia - https://en.wikipedia.org/wiki/Visa_policy_of_Kenya

Citizens of 43 countries can visit Kenya without a visa for up to 90 days, including many African and Caribbean nations, as well as selected Asian nations (Brunei, Malaysia, Singapore).

## Madagascar

Government website - http://www.evisamada.gov.mg/en_US/
Wikipedia - https://en.wikipedia.org/wiki/Visa_policy_of_Madagascar

All visitors to Madagascar are required to obtain a visa in advance of their journey.

## Morocco

Government website - https://www.consulat.ma/en/ordinary-visas
Wikipedia - https://en.wikipedia.org/wiki/Visa_policy_of_Morocco

Citizens of 69 countries can enter Morocco visa-free for up to 90 days, including European Union, many countries of the Americas, several Asian nations (Australia, China, Hong Kong, Indonesia, Japan, Malaysia, New Zealand, Philippines, Singapore, South Korea).

## Namibia

Government website - http://www.mha.gov.na/web/mhai/visas-immigration-control-act-act-no-7
Wikipedia - https://en.wikipedia.org/wiki/Visa_policy_of_Namibia

Namibia offers 55 countries visa-free access for up to 90 days, including most European countries, some Asian nations (Australia, Hong Kong, Indonesia, Japan, Malaysia, New Zealand, Singapore), Canada, and United States.

## South Africa

Government website - https://www.gov.za/services/temporary-residence/visa
Wikipedia - https://en.wikipedia.org/wiki/Visa_policy_of_South_Africa

Citizens of 76 countries are able to enter South Africa visa-free for 30 to 90 days, depending on nationality. This includes most Western European nations, the majority of the Americas, many Asian nations (Australia, Hong Kong, Japan, Malaysia, Singapore, South Korea, Thailand).

# BEST TIME OF THE YEAR FOR TRAVEL

Sometimes you want to escape to somewhere to take photos of empty beaches, quiet streets, and the enviable laid-back life that draws some people to your preferred destination. Or, you want to be amongst the action, capturing the hustle and bustle of daily life, or the invasion of the tourists. Here is the broad overview of the weather that you can expect in different parts of the world. The busiest times tend to revolve around the hottest months, as it is when locals tend to escape the heat and trade places with the tourists. Cold months (as noted below) coincide with snow and / or temperatures at freezing point or below.

## Americas

### Northern America

- Hot months - July, August
- Cold months - December to March

### Southern United States / Mexico

- Hot months - May to September
- Cold months - None (barring the occasional light snow)

## Central America

- Hot months - May to September
- Cold months - None
- Wet season - May to November

## South America

- Hot months - December to March
- Cold months - June to September

# Asia

## Australia

- Hot months - November to April
- Cold months - June to September

## China (North)

- Hot months - July and August
- Cold months - December to March
- Wet months - July and August

## China (South)

- Hot months - July and August
- Cold months - January to March
- Wet months - May to September

## India

- Hot months - June to September
- Cold months - None (except towards the Himalayas)
- Wet months - July to September

## Japan

- Hot months - July and August
- Cold months - January to March
- Wet months - August to November

## New Zealand

- Hot months - December to March
- Cold months - June to September

### South East Asia

- Hot months - June to October
- Cold months - None
- Wet months - May to October

# Europe

### British Isles (including Ireland)

- Hot months - July and August
- Cold months - December to March
- Wet months - Year-round (depending on who you ask!)

### Eastern / Western Europe

- Hot months - July and August
- Cold months - December to March
- Wet months - September to October

### Mediterranean

- Hot months - June to September
- Cold months - January and February
- Wet months - February to April, October and November

### Nordics

- Hot months - July and August
- Cold months - November to April

# Africa

### North Africa

- Hot months - June to September
- Cold months - January and February

### East Africa

- Hot months - June to September
- Cold months - None
- Wettest months - March to May

# West Africa

- Hot months - November to April
- Cold months - None
- Wettest months - May to July, September and October

# HEALTH

## GENERAL HEALTH PRECAUTIONS

### Vaccinations

Having the appropriate vaccinations prior to travel to certain parts of the world manages the risk of infection. In some countries, there are mandatory vaccination requirements, particularly if you have recently visited some Asian, African, or South American destinations. Here are some helpful sites that tell you what vaccinations to get when travelling:

#### World Health Organisation (WHO) recommendations

Website - https://www.who.int/ith/vaccines/en/

Some countries require a vaccination certificate against some diseases for travellers who are entering their country. In the same way, the WHO advises travellers to countries which are known to have a risk of contracting highly contagious and dangerous diseases, such as MERS-CoV and yellow fever, to get the proper vaccination before travelling. In addition, the website describes other precautions to take, including avoiding crowded places, stagnant water, etc.

#### Additional information

- TravelVax - https://www.travelvax.com.au/holiday-traveller/vaccination-requirements
- United States Centres for Disease Control and Prevention - https://wwwnc.cdc.gov/travel

#### Hepatitis A and B

Hepatitis is an inflammation of the liver. Hepatitis A usually comes from eating infected food. Fortunately, you can recover from Hepatitis A over time. Hepatitis B, on the other hand, can be acute and chronic because it spreads through the blood. This type of hepatitis is common in Asia and Africa. Despite this, both types of hepatitis can be prevented by vaccination.

#### Whooping cough

Whooping cough or pertussis is a bacterial infection that enters through your nose or throat. Symptoms of the infection includes low fever, sneezing, mild coughing, and runny nose. The cough can turn into coughing spells after 7 to 10 days. Preventative vaccines include DTaP and Tdap.

## Polio

Polio is a deadly infectious disease which can spread from person to person. When the virus enters the body, it can attack the brain and the spinal cord causing paralysis. Polio can be prevented by vaccination – oral poliovirus vaccine (OPV) and inactivated poliovirus vaccine (IPV) which is injected in the arm or leg.

# Tropical diseases

## Cholera

Cholera is a highly infectious and deadly disease characterised by watery diarrhoea. When left untreated, this can lead to dehydration, or even death. Cholera is caused by a bacterium found in dirty food or contaminated drinking water. There is a vaccine against cholera however the WHO and CDC normally don't recommend this because the protection is short-lived. Rather, they advise using only bottled or boiled water in almost everything during your travel and avoiding eating raw food or unpeeled fruits and vegetables.

## Malaria

Malaria is a life-threatening disease characterised by high fever, headache, shaking chills, profuse sweating, nausea, abdominal pain, and vomiting. There is no vaccine to prevent malaria, however prescribed medication is available to help prevent contracting malaria. You are advised to consult your doctor if you are travelling to an area where the risk of malaria is high.

## Typhoid

Typhoid fever is an acute illness caused by a type of salmonella virus. It is usually contracted from contaminated food and water. There are two types of vaccine used to prevent typhoid fever – an oral vaccine, and an injectable given in a single dose.

## Yellow fever

Yellow fever is caused by infected mosquitoes and is characterised by chills and fever, as well as muscle aches and headaches. It can be prevented by a vaccine administered as a single shot.

## Zika virus

The zika virus has come into common awareness due to recent outbreaks. It is contracted from mosquitos, or exchange of bodily fluids (including blood). Symptoms include fever, headache, rash, joint or muscle pain, and red eyes. Zika is of particularly high risk to pregnant women (or women looking to get pregnant), as Zika has been linked to birth defects.

# Other recommended vaccinations

## Rabies

Rabies is a viral disease contracted when bitten by a rabid animal. When you get bitten by a suspected rabid animal, thoroughly wash the bitten part with soap and water. There are more than 150 countries where rabies is present, and travellers are advised to seek urgent medical attention if they believe that they may have been infected by a rabid animal (dogs are the most likely culprit).

## Japanese encephalitis

It is caused by a disease spread by an infected mosquito. Symptoms usually develop between 5 and 15 days. These symptoms include fever, headache, and vomiting. The disease can be prevented by vaccination, the vaccine of which is given in two doses given four weeks apart. If you are travelling to areas prone to this disease, you are advised to take a vaccine six months prior to your departure.

# Drinkable water

Water is a necessity for our continued existence, and if you live in a "developed" country you can often take it for granted that you are able to drink water straight out of the tap. This is something that can take a bit of adaption when traveling to parts of the world where such relative luxuries are not available. Here are some general tips to help you stay hydrated and avoid becoming sick on your travels:

## Know the local water quality ahead of time

This may feel obvious however it never hurts to be armed with good information as soon as possible. The United States Center of Disease Control and Prevention (CDC) has a handy travel website that can give you more information about drinkable water (https://wwwnc.cdc.gov/travel/).

## Don't be a hero

Some people believe that they have an "iron stomach", or that because they didn't have any issues 20 years ago in a country they are going to be fine today. This can include people who have emigrated from one country to another, and so have been out of the previous country for some time. Your stomach environment changes over time and adapts to your local surroundings. This means that previous "tolerances" that you may have possessed will deteriorate over time.

Err on the side of caution if there's any doubt.

## Buy bottled water before you need it

When you arrive into a new place, particularly a new country, chances are that you will be paying over the odds for bottled water in an airport or central train station. Despite this, it is a good strategy to pay a little bit more for a smaller bottle of water as soon as you have an opportunity, as you may not be able to get access to water again for several hours.

Imagine arriving late into the evening (or night) at your destination, and by the time you get to your hotel accommodation, all of the local shops in the area are closed. If your hotel room (or the lobby) doesn't have water available, you will have to wait for the following morning in order to get something to drink. This risk applies even more if you are staying in private accommodation.

## Buy more water than you think you'll need

Building a little bit on the point above, having more water than you expect to consume is hardly a big issue, especially if you buy bigger bottle sizes. In the worst case, you can leave the spare bottles in the accommodation you are staying in for the next guest. Or, you can ask a homeless person if they would like the water – you're hardly likely to be turned down!

## Photography is thirsty work

Walking about all day, including carrying all of those extra lenses that you swore you'd need, all saps your body of energy and fluid. Aim to consume at very least two litres of water per day, excluding any water that you'll take in through food / other drinks.

## Be wary of ice and water provided in glasses

A prudent strategy when traveling to places that don't have good quality water supplies is to avoid ice in your drinks. Sometimes the water used for ice blocks will come from a tap rather from a filtered source and can cause issues for you once melted. This applies for soft drinks (fizzy drinks / soda / pop), shakes, smoothies, or alcoholic beverages.

When served water served in glasses / cups, ask the wait staff whether the water comes from a filtered source. If in doubt, politely decline the water. As a rule, higher-end establishments do serve filtered water, however it always is a good to ask first.

## Options for when things get a little desperate

Your body is going to start becoming dehydrated before you actually feel thirsty. The following suggestions are for those times when drinkable water isn't readily available:

- **Purification tablets -** Whilst not guaranteed to be 100% safe, purification tablets are quite compact and have a very long shelf life (several years). The trick is to remember to pack them in the first place!

- **Boiling water -** If your hotel room / accommodation has an electric jug, or even a saucepan and stove, you can boil water. Make sure that you keep the water boiling for at least 10 minutes (somewhat tricky with an electric jug). Ideally, scoop off the top layer of water, or pour the top of the contents out. In any case, drink the minimum amount of water that will tide you over until you can access proper drinkable water.

- **Soft drinks** - The quality standards of recognisable brands such as Coca Cola and PepsiCo are universal. Theses brand drinks are safe to drink anywhere in the world, provided you are drinking from an unopened can / bottle.

- **Beer -** Hardly the greatest hydration strategy, however it is included here for completeness. Beer used to be consumed in the Middle Ages in Europe in place of water, as the water wasn't fit for drinking. Apply the same standards to beer as to soft drinks, and only drink from a can or bottle that you've opened yourself (or seen opened). For tap beer, inspect the surface of the tap and get a general sense if the glasses are cleaned appropriately. Note that beer (or other low alcohol content drinks) is a stop-gap solution and is by no means a replacement for water! Chances are, if you can get access to beer, you can get access to drinkable water.

# HYGIENE

Keeping your body in top shape is most important when you are out of your regular environment. Putting aside the extra exercise associated with taking photos, your body will be grappling with new foods and tastes, and whatever is in the local air.

## Personal care

The tips below are provided for the little facets of life that we take for granted each day, and we sometimes tend to forget about how a change in environment could affect these almost unconscious tasks.

### Showering

As per the tips above about drinking water, apply the same logic to ingesting water when showering. Keep your mouth closed when showering, and otherwise go about your business as usual.

Many countries have manual hot water boilers (often called geysers) that will need to be switched on in advance of your shower. Generally heating the water to the desired temperature can take 5-15 minutes. Don't forget to switch off the geyser when you are finished with the hot water, as they tend to use large amounts of electricity.

### Cleaning teeth

The prudent approach is to use a cup of bottled water to clean your teeth. However, so long as you don't consume the water when cleaning (or rinsing), using tap water can mostly be considered okay.

### Squat toilets

Squat toilets are quite common throughout Asia and Africa and tend to be more common in countries that have a predominantly Muslim or Hindu population. They are generally more sanitary than Western-style toilets, as the person doesn't make skin contact with the toilet when using them. Cleaning yourself is typically with a water source nearby (a hose, or a bucket of water), and so toilet paper may not be available. Make sure you check for toilet paper before you commence proceedings!

If you have not used one of these types of toilet, it is advisable to read up on the logistics involved (https://en.wikipedia.org/wiki/Squat_toilet) before getting involved. In some places, there are even signs that are posted explaining the appropriate use of the toilet, which can often appear funny to Western minds not used to such activities.

## Existing medication

As discussed previously (page 35), don't forget to take your medication with you! It's strongly advisable to carry any medication in your carry-on baggage just in case you get delayed to your destination (or home). Carry extra medication beyond the number of days that you'll be away, if possible.

## Allergies

Managing allergies to food items whilst on the road can be challenging, particularly if you are going to a destination where you don't speak the language. To help navigate menus and cuisines, try to have your allergies translated into the local language and have it written down. You can use services such as Google Translate (https://translate.google.com/) or ask somebody at the reception in your hotel to write it down for you.

## Sleep

Depending on the length of your trip, you may find that your sleep is interrupted by the new location (and potentially time zone). If you have trouble sleeping because of noise, consider taking ear plugs with you to help get a good night's sleep.

## Jet lag

There are plenty of suggestions available that help you manage the symptoms of jet lag, however a sure-fire cure has yet to be revealed. If you do know the secret to avoiding jet lag, please write to us!

# First-aid kit items

The items below can help you ensure a quick and smooth response to medical hiccups that are bound to happen from time to time. These are in addition to carrying toiletries (page 56).

## Essential items

The good news about the items below is that they are largely compact in size and weight and are readily available in pharmacies around the world (including airports).

- **Plasters** - Treatment for small cuts as well as for abrasions on your feet (or other body parts) from walking.

- **Sun cream** - Sun burn and sun stroke can be painful and cause longer term damage (page 55).

- **Hand sanitiser** - Generally helpful, particularly if you are coming in regular contact with unhygienic surfaces.

- **Antiseptic cream** - Helps protect against infection from cuts and abrasions.

- **Antihistamine** - Over-the-counter treatment of mild allergies.

- **Anti-diarrheal** - Using the active ingredient loperamide, useful for management of diarrhoea. This is particularly useful if you have to travel somewhere, or don't have ready access to toilet facilities.

- **Insect repellent** - For keeping the bugs at bay. Included under the "essentials" list because when you need it, you need it!

- **Paracetamol** - Pain relief from mild pain and fever.

## Good to have

These items will help you deal with less common issues that are still likely to come up. These items can generally be purchased from a pharmacy, however there may be a little greater language challenge:

- **Portable respirator face mask** - For managing smoggy or polluted environments, as well as dust storms. Ideally an N95 or greater rating can provide reasonable protection. Note that paper face masks aren't effective for extended periods of time.

- **Activated carbon pills** - Also known as activated charcoal, this can be used to help treat suspected mild poisoning (i.e. food poisoning) as well as management of diarrhoea.

- **Aspirin** - Similar effects to paracetamol, as well as treatment of mild swelling and inflammation.

- **Aloe vera cream** - For treatment of sunburn.

- **Small sewing kit** - Not strictly medically-related, a small sewing kit (the kind often found in hotel bathrooms) can help repair small fabric tears and sew on button in case of emergency.

# WALKABOUT PHOTO GUIDES

## ABOUT US

Walkabout photo guides was founded with the express mission of enabling budding travel photographers to get out and explore new places and come home with great photos!

We combine experience on the ground with extensive research, distilling it into a coherent structure, saving the reader hours of time. Our guides enable the reader to confidently be on top of the logistics of a trip focused on taking photos (which is often different to a holiday).

No matter whether you're a weekend warrior, digital nomad, or first-time traveller, our guides will shortcut a lot of the planning and logistics that can stand in the way of getting great travel photos.

# ABOUT THE AUTHOR

James Dugan was born and raised in Australia. The travel bug bit him on his first trip overseas to India aged 13. He has since visited over 60 countries. After university, James embarked on a career that saw him based in London, Sydney, Singapore, and New York. During this time, weekends and holidays were spent traveling extensively and exploring the surrounding areas. Photography became a passion early on as a way of capturing these travels, and as a creative outlet to balance against corporate life. It also became a way to inspire and encourage others, stuck in their cubicles, to get out and explore. This book draws on these experiences and paying forward the help and support received over the years.

## James's thanks

A huge thanks to my family and friends for encouraging me during the writing of this guide. In particular, fellow travel companions and those who shared their ideas, tips, and feedback: Tendai Gomo, Carlos Lopez, Reshma Varghese, Sarah O'Toole, Arunjay Katakam, Line Sagfors, and Vinay Dugan.

Printed in Great Britain
by Amazon